Betty Crocker's Microwaving for One or Two

Betty Crocker's
Microwaving
for One or Two

Random House, Inc. New York

Take any one or two people — a single, a couple or apartment mates — with little time to cook but a love for good food. Add one microwave and this book of up-to-date microwave information and all-new recipes. The result: delicious meals in minutes — enjoyed at leisure!

BETTY CROCKER'S MICROWAVING FOR ONE OR TWO contains 128 pages of more than 185 recipes for favorite and unusual foods and is liberally illustrated with more than 75 color photographs. Here are recipes for Hearty Main Dishes and Mini-Main Dishes. Side Dishes include a sparkling array of vegetable combinations, both fresh and frozen, and Breads, savory to sweet. Finally, there are Snacks and Sweets from appetizers to dessert sauces tailored specially to today's more casual tastes and eating habits. Recipes appear in a unique format, listing ingredients for one serving, then in a second column for two, plus microwave timing directions noted separately for one or two. Clear, concise and easy to follow, all recipes were developed and thoroughly tested in the Betty Crocker Kitchens.

For the first-time microwave owner, a Technical Section supplies basic information followed by practical advice on microwave utensils and techniques, tips on making the most of the microwave, and on shopping and storage for food in small quantities. Charts of microwaving terms and techniques, for timing fresh and frozen vegetables and for reheating main dishes and breads, ensure expert results.

So if you have — or know — a household of one or two replete with a microwave, this is the perfect addition. It fulfills the promise of good and interesting food with absolutely no slaving over a hot stove!

Editor, De Abbott; Recipe Development Editors, Ginny Allen, Mary Jane Friedhoff; Copy Editor, Kris Schwappach; Copywriter, Elizabeth Lemmer; Food Styling Coordinator, Cindy Lund; Food Stylists, Carol Grones, Linel Polesky, Mary Sethre; Art Director, Lynne Dolan; Prop Styling, Gail Bailey; Photographer, Steven Smith

Library of Congress Cataloging in Publication Data   Crocker, Betty. Betty Crocker's Microwaving for One or Two.

1. Microwave cookery. I. Title. II. Title: Microwaving for One or Two.
TX832.C77   1985   641.5'882   84-45775

Manufactured in the United States of America   4689753

ISBN 0-394-53593-6

Contents

Tips & Techniques

Using the Recipes in This Book

The ingredients for the recipes in this book are listed in two columns. The first column lists ingredients for one serving. The second column lists ingredients for two servings and appears in bold type. The instructions for preparing the recipe are given for both one and two servings; however, directions that refer specifically to two servings always appear in brackets and bold type.

Southwest-Style Chili

1 Serving	[2 Servings]	
½ cup coarsely chopped cooked beef (3 oz)	**1 cup coarsely chopped beef (6 oz)**	——— Brackets for 2 servings
½ cup mild salsa	**1 cup mild salsa**	
¼ cup water	**½ cup water**	
1 tsp cornmeal	**2 tsp cornmeal**	Bold type for 2 servings
⅛ tsp ground cumin	**¼ tsp ground cumin**	
Dash of crushed dried hot chilies, if desired	**⅛ tsp crushed dried hot chilies, if desired**	

Mix all ingredients in 16-oz casserole [**1-qt casserole**]. Cover loosely and microwave on high (550 watts) 1 min; stir. Cover loosely and microwave until hot, 1 to 2 min longer [**3 to 5 min longer**]. Serve with hot pinto beans and hot cooked rice if desired.

——— Brackets for 2 servings

——— Brackets for 2 servings

Testing for This Book

These recipes were tested in the Betty Crocker Kitchens using countertop microwaves with power outputs of 500 to 700 watts. Refer to the use and care booklet that came with your microwave or contact the manufacturer to learn what the wattages are for each setting on your microwave. Then, if the settings on your microwave do not correspond (approximately) with the watts listed in the chart below, microwave the dishes in this book according to the watts (not the settings) referred to in each recipe.

Microwave Setting	Approximate Watts	Percentage of Power Output
High	550	100
Medium-high	385	70
Medium	275	50
Medium-low	165	30
Low	55	10

Special features and accessories (browning grill, microwave shelf, temperature probe, memory, etc.) vary among brands of microwaves. Consult your use and care booklet for guidelines on how to use these special features.

Microwaving Tips

Blanching

Almonds

Place ½ cup water in small bowl. Microwave uncovered on high (550 watts) until boiling, 1½ to 2½ min. Add ¼ cup whole natural almonds, Microwave uncovered until skin is soft, 30 to 45 sec. Drain hot water from bowl; cover almonds with cold water. Pinch each nut between thumb and finger to push off skin; spread almonds on plate to dry.

Heating

Finger Towels

Place two dampened rolled finger towels on small plate. Microwave uncovered on high (550 watts) until hot, 45 to 60 sec.

Ice-cream Toppings

Place ¼ cup ice-cream topping in 1-cup measure. Microwave uncovered on high (550 watts) until warm, 15 to 30 sec; stir.

Syrups

Place ¼ cup syrup in small pitcher or 1-cup measure. Microwave uncovered on high (550 watts) until warm, 20 to 30 sec.

Melting

Caramels

Place 24 caramel candies (7 oz) and 1 tbsp water in 10-oz custard cup. Microwave uncovered on high (550 watts), stirring every 30 sec, until melted, 1½ to 2½ min; stir until smooth.

Chocolate Chips

Place ¼ cup chocolate chips in 6-oz custard cup. Microwave uncovered on medium (275 watts) until softened, 1 to 1½ min; stir until smooth.

Chocolate Squares

Place 1 square (1 oz) chocolate in 6-oz custard cup. Microwave uncovered on medium (275 watts) 1 min; stir. Microwave uncovered until softened, 30 to 60 sec longer.

Miscellaneous

Opening Oysters

Scrub 6 oysters in shells under running cold water. Arrange oysters on plate with hinges toward outside. Cover tightly and microwave on high (550 watts) until shells open slightly, 1 to 1½ min. (Remove oysters as they begin to open.) Open by holding oyster with hinge toward you. Insert oyster knife between shells near hinge; twist knife and pull shells apart. Cut oyster at muscle to separate from shell.

Softening

Brown Sugar

Cover tightly and microwave on high (550 watts), checking every 30 sec, until softened.

Cream Cheese

Remove foil wrapper from 3-oz pkg of cream cheese and place in bowl. Microwave uncovered on medium (275 watts) until softened, 30 to 45 sec. (Cheese will hold its shape as it softens.)

Hard Ice Cream

Remove the cover from 1 pint of solidly frozen ice cream; place pint of ice cream in carton on plate. Cover with plastic wrap and microwave on high (550 watts) until softened, 10 to 15 sec.

Margarine or Butter

Microwave margarine or butter uncovered on serving dish on medium-low (165 watts), checking every 10 sec, until softened.

Toasting

Almonds

Place 2 tbsp sliced almonds and 1 tsp margarine in 6-oz custard cup. Microwave uncovered on high (550 watts), stirring every 30 sec, until almonds are light brown, 3 to 4 min. Watch carefully to prevent overmicrowaving.

Bread Crumbs

Toss ½ cup soft bread crumbs (about 1 slice bread) and ½ tsp margarine or butter, melted, in pie plate. Microwave uncovered on high (550 watts), stirring every 30 sec, until dried, 1 to 1¼ min.

Coconut

Place ¼ cup flaked or shredded coconut in pie plate. Microwave uncovered on high (550 watts), stirring every 30 sec, until toasted, 30 to 45 sec. Watch carefully to prevent overmicrowaving.

Croutons

Arrange ½ cup ½" bread cubes in pie plate. Microwave uncovered on high (550 watts) 1 min; stir. Microwave uncovered until dry, 30 to 60 sec longer.

Warming

Fruit (for easier squeezing)

Place 1 orange or lemon in microwave oven. Microwave uncovered on medium-low (165 watts) until warm, 20 to 30 sec.

Liquor (for flaming)

Place 2 tbsp liquor in 1-cup measure. Microwave uncovered on high (550 watts) until warm, 15 to 20 sec. Fill metal ladle or serving spoon with liquor; ignite and pour over warm fruit.

Microwaving Terms and Techniques

Arrange: Foods such as muffins or potatoes cook more evenly in a circle because all sides of food are exposed to equal amounts of microwaves.

Coat: Foods such as chicken or fish can be coated with paprika or crumbs before microwaving to add color, crispness and flavor.

Cover loosely: Use waxed paper or casserole lid slightly ajar to allow some moisture and steam to escape and to reduce spattering.

Cover tightly: Use casserole lid, plate or vented plastic wrap to speed cooking and reduce spattering in microwave.

Cover with vented plastic wrap: Use plastic wrap with one corner or edge turned back to prevent wrap from splitting.

Elevate: Foods such as quiche or Impossible Pie should be microwaved on an inverted dinner plate or on a rack so that bottom center can absorb microwaves to ensure doneness.

Let stand: Foods such as meats, layered casseroles and some vegetables require standing time after microwaving (see individual recipes) to complete cooking and develop the flavor.

Prick: Foods such as egg yolks, potatoes or squash should be pricked with fork before microwaving to prevent bursting.

Rearrange: Reposition food in dish so that it cooks more evenly. This technique is important for food that cannot be stirred, such as kabobs.

Reheat: Foods that need long reheat times should be placed at the outside edge of the dish, and foods that need shorter reheat times (such as a roll or muffin) should be placed in the center or added later for a brief time. Spread food out, add sauce or gravy and cover to heat evenly.

Rotate: A dish can be rotated ¼ or ½ turn, as directed in recipes. Foods that cannot be stirred, such as asparagus or broccoli spears, cook more evenly when dish is rotated.

Stir: Always stir from outside to center to distribute heat and help food cook more quickly and evenly. Food heats and cooks faster on the outside.

Temperature: An instant thermometer should be used to test the doneness of some foods toward the end of microwaving. Insert stainless-steel stem horizontally into the center of pork or fish to give a quick and accurate reading on degree of doneness of food. Do not leave thermometer in food during microwaving.

Turn over: Foods such as small roasts or pork chops should be turned over from top to bottom for even cooking.

Microwavable Utensils

Many of the recipes in this book are mixed, microwaved and served in one small casserole. Check your kitchen for microwavable utensils that are suitable size for small amounts of food because a small quantity of food may not microwave well in a utensil that is too large. Use oven-tempered glass, plasticware, dishwasher-safe plastic containers, ceramic plates, paper plates and casseroles that contain no metals, and china that has no metal trim. Do not use metal utensils. Follow your microwave manufacturer's directions for using aluminum foil or foil-lined containers.

Microwavable Utensil	Size for 1 Serving	Size for [2 Servings]
Casserole	10, 12, 13, 14, 15, 16 oz	**20, 21, 22, 24, 26 oz 1, 1½ qt**
Custard Cup	6, 10 oz	
Loaf dish	7 × 4¾ × 1", 6¼ × 5¼ × 1½"	**7½ × 3¾ × 2¼"**
Measure	1 cup	**2, 4 cup**
Pie plate	4¼ × 1¼, 5 × 1"	**6 × 1, 8 × 1¼, 9 × 1¼"**
Rack	rack to fit rectangular dish (bacon rack, roasting rack)	
Rectangular dish		**10 × 6 × 1½, 11 × 7 × 1½"**
Ring dish	2½ cup	**5 cup**
Round dish		**8 × 1½"**
Square dish		**8 × 8 × 2"**
Soup bowl	12, 15 oz	
Quiche dish	10 oz	
Au gratin dish	14 oz	

Shopping and Storage

More markets are recognizing the existence of the one- or two-member household, so look for individual servings of prepackaged meats, poultry or seafood, or purchase small amounts from your "over the counter" meat dealer. Fruits and vegetables can be purchased by the piece in many markets. Also don't forget the deli sections of supermarkets; they are good places to find just-for-one buys. If canned goods are on your list, the 8-oz can sizes are definitely for you. They may cost more, but you'll eliminate unwanted leftovers. The freezer section also offers a large selection of single-serving main dishes, side dishes and multicourse dinners. Many freezer selections have microwave directions on the package. Date the package so the food is used before it begins to lose some of its moisture, flavor or texture. The following chart will serve as a guideline on quantities to purchase for one or two people. Increase the amount for hearty appetites.

Food	Amount to Purchase for 1 or [2 Servings]	Storage Tips
Bread	Purchase in small quantities. See also Bread Reheat Chart (page 107).	Store wrapped 5 to 7 days. Bread (baked) can be frozen 2 to 3 months.
Cheese Cream Hard Sliced Spread	 3 oz 6 to 8 oz 6 to 8 oz 5 to 8 oz	Refrigerate cream cheese tightly covered 2 weeks. Wrap hard cheese tightly; refrigerate up to 2 months (discard if moldy). Refrigerate cheese slices and spreads, covered tightly, 1 to 2 weeks after opening. Cream cheese is not recommended for freezing. Freeze other cheeses in small amounts, wrapped tightly, for 3 to 4 months; thaw in refrigerator to prevent crumbling.
Eggs, fresh	1 dozen or ½ dozen (from specialty stores)	Refrigerate 1 week with the large ends up. Eggs can be refrigerated longer, but expect loss of some quality and flavor.
Fish and Seafood fish steaks fish fillets	 about 3 oz per serving about 3 oz per serving	Refrigerate in plastic wrap or waxed paper 1 to 2 days. Fatty fish (salmon, trout) wrapped airtight can be frozen 3 to 4 months, lean fish (cod, haddock, halibut) 6 to 8 months. Seafood (lobster or scallops) wrapped airtight can be frozen 1 to 2 months. Shellfish wrapped airtight can be frozen 3 to 4 months.
Fruit	Purchase by the piece or in small quantities	Store most fruit uncovered in the refrigerator. Apples can be refrigerated up to 1 month; citrus fruit up to 2 weeks. Apricots, avocados, bananas, melons, peaches, pears and plums should be stored at room temperature until ripe and then refrigerated from 3 to 5 days. Peel on bananas will darken in refrigerator. Berries, cherries and pineapple can be refrigerated 2 to 3 days.

Shopping & Storage (continued)

Food	Amount to Purchase for 1 or [2 Servings]	Storage Tips
Meat, fresh boneless small bone-in	about 4 oz per serving about 5 oz per serving	Cover loosely and refrigerate 1 to 3 days. Ground meat and variety meat should not be refrigerated more than 24 hours before using. Beef, veal or lamb roasts or steaks wrapped airtight can be frozen 8 to 12 months. Ground beef or stew meat wrapped airtight can be frozen 2 to 3 months. Fresh pork wrapped airtight can be frozen 4 to 6 months.
Meat, processed cold cuts bacon frankfurters ham, canned ham, sliced	about 4 oz per serving 8-oz package (2 strips per serving) 12-oz package (2 per serving) 1½ lb can (3 oz per serving) 12-oz slice (3 oz per serving)	Refrigerate in original wrapper and reseal after opening. Cold cuts can be refrigerated 2 weeks (unopened) or 3 to 5 days (opened). Bacon or frankfurters can be refrigerated 1 week or frozen 1 to 2 months (wrap airtight). Canned ham can be refrigerated 1 year (unopened) and 5 days (opened). Ham slice can be refrigerated 3 days. Cured pork loses desirable color and flavor during freezer storage.
Pasta, rice or noodles	5, 6, 7, 8, 10-oz packages	Store pasta and rice in tightly closed container at room temperature up to 1 year, noodles and seasoned rice mixes up to 6 months.
Poultry, pieces	about 3 oz per serving	Refrigerate in plastic wrap or waxed paper 1 to 2 days or freeze 4 to 6 months (wrap airtight). Giblets can be frozen 1 to 3 months.
Sandwiches		Wrap sandwiches tightly; freeze up to 1 month. Do not freeze sandwiches with fillings made from mayonnaise, salad dressing, jelly, fresh vegetables or cooked egg whites.
Soups and stews		Cover and refrigerate 3 to 4 days. Freeze in small portions for 2 to 3 months.
Vegetables	Purchase in small quantities. See also Frozen Vegetable Microwaving Chart (page 87) or Fresh Vegetable Microwaving Chart (page 85)	Store most vegetables in crisper drawer of refrigerator in plastic bags 3 to 5 days. Asparagus and sweet corn are very perishable. Refrigerate asparagus (unwashed) 2 to 3 days, corn (unhusked and uncovered) for only 1 day. Lettuce and greens should be washed and drained; refrigerate 5 to 7 days. Tomatoes can be refrigerated (uncovered) up to 1 week. Remove tops of root vegetables and refrigerate in plastic bags up to 2 weeks. Onions (dry), potatoes and winter squash keep best in a cool, dry place for up to 2 months. Commercially frozen vegetables can be stored at 0° for up to 8 months.

Hearty Main Dishes

Roast Beef Strips

1 Serving	[2 Servings]
3 oz cooked beef roast, cut into thin strips (3/4 cup)	6 oz cooked beef roast, cut into thin strips (1½ cups)
2 tbsp dry red wine	¼ cup dry red wine
2 tsp margarine or butter	1 tbsp margarine or butter
1/8 tsp salt	¼ tsp salt
Dash of garlic powder	1/8 tsp garlic powder
5 drops red pepper sauce	10 drops red pepper sauce
½ small green pepper, cut into ¼" strips	1 small green pepper, cut into ¼" strips
1/8" slice medium onion, separated into rings	Two 1/8" slices medium onion, separated into rings
1 small tomato, cut into wedges	1 large tomato, cut into wedges
3/4 cup hot cooked rice	1½ cups hot cooked rice

Mix all ingredients except tomato and rice in 21-oz casserole [1-qt casserole]. Cover tightly and microwave on high (550 watts) 1½ to 2½ min [2½ to 3½ min]. Stir in tomato. Microwave uncovered until hot, 1½ to 2 min [2 to 3 min]. Serve over rice.

One-Rib Roast

1 Serving	[2 Servings]
Prepare One-Rib Roast with Tomato Slices for 2 Servings. Reheat half of the beef for another meal. See Main Dish Reheat Chart, page 83.	2 tbsp margarine or butter, melted
	½ tsp browning sauce
	1/8 tsp garlic powder
	1/8 tsp paprika
	1- lb beef rib roast (1 rib cut from small end), 1" thick
	1 large tomato, cut into 4 slices

Mix margarine, browning sauce, garlic powder and paprika. Brush over both sides of beef and 1 side of each tomato slice. Place beef on center of rack in 11 × 7 × 1½" dish. Cover with waxed paper and microwave on medium-low (165 watts) 5 min; rotate dish ½ turn. Place tomato slices on rack around beef. Cover with waxed paper and microwave until meat thermometer inserted horizontally in beef registers 140°, 6 to 10 min. Cover beef with aluminum foil; let stand 5 min. To serve, spoon beef juices over carved beef. Sprinkle tomato slices with snipped parsley if desired.

Beef Slices, Sauerbraten Style

1 Serving	[2 Servings]
1½ tsp margarine or butter	1 tbsp margarine or butter
1 tsp all-purpose flour	2 tsp all-purpose flour
¼ cup dry red wine	½ cup dry red wine
¼ cup water	½ cup water
1 tsp packed brown sugar	2 tsp packed brown sugar
¼ tsp browning sauce	½ tsp browning sauce
⅛ tsp salt	¼ tsp salt
Dash of ground cloves	Dash of ground cloves
Freshly ground pepper	Freshly ground pepper
1 gingersnap, crushed (1 tbsp plus 1 tsp)	2 gingersnaps, crushed (2 tbsp)
3 oz cooked beef roast, thinly sliced	6 oz cooked beef roast, thinly sliced
⅛" slice medium onion, separated into rings	Two ⅛" slices medium onion, separated into rings
¾ cup hot cooked noodles	1½ cups hot cooked noodles

Microwave margarine uncovered in 21-oz casserole [1-qt casserole] on high (550 watts) until melted, about 30 sec [about 45 sec]. Mix in flour. Stir in remaining ingredients except beef, onion and noodles. Microwave uncovered, stirring every min, until thickened, 1 to 1½ min [2 to 3 min]. Add beef and onion; spoon sauce over top. Cover loosely and microwave until onion is crisp-tender and beef is hot, 2 to 3 min [4 to 5 min]. Serve over hot noodles.

Beef Tenderloin with Basil Mushrooms

1 Serving	[2 Servings]
2 tsp margarine or butter, melted	1 tbsp plus 1 tsp margarine or butter, melted
¼ tsp browning sauce	½ tsp browning sauce
1 slice (4 oz) beef tenderloin (¾" thick)	2 slices (4 oz each) beef tenderloin (¾" thick)
3 large mushrooms, stems removed	6 large mushrooms, stems removed
⅛ tsp dried basil leaves	¼ tsp dried basil leaves

Mix margarine and browning sauce. Brush half of the margarine mixture over both sides of beef tenderloin. Place beef on rack in 11 × 7 × 1½" dish. Cover with waxed paper and microwave on medium (275 watts) 3 min [5 min]; rotate dish ½ turn. Place mushrooms on rack around beef; brush with remaining margarine mixture and sprinkle with basil. Cover with waxed paper and microwave until meat thermometer inserted horizontally in beef registers 135°, 2 to 3 min [1 to 3 min]. Spoon beef juices over beef and, if desired, sprinkle with salt and pepper. Sprinkle mushrooms with grated Parmesan cheese if desired.

Southwest-Style Chili

1 Serving	[2 Servings]
½ cup coarsely chopped cooked beef (3 oz)	1 cup coarsely chopped beef (6 oz)
½ cup mild salsa	1 cup mild salsa
¼ cup water	½ cup water
1 tsp cornmeal	2 tsp cornmeal
⅛ tsp ground cumin	¼ tsp ground cumin
Dash of crushed dried hot chilies, if desired	⅛ tsp crushed dried hot chilies, if desired

Mix all ingredients in 16-oz casserole [1-qt casserole]. Cover loosely and microwave on high (550 watts) 1 min; stir. Cover loosely and microwave until hot, 1 to 2 min longer [3 to 5 min longer]. Serve with hot pinto beans and hot cooked rice if desired.

Beef Tenderloin with Basil Mushrooms

Stuffed Beef Rolls

1 Serving	[2 Servings]
¼- lb beef boneless sirloin steak (½" thick)	½- lb beef boneless sirloin steak (½" thick), cut into halves
½ cup cooked long grain and wild rice mix	1 cup cooked long grain and wild rice mix
2 tsp grated Parmesan cheese	1 tbsp grated Parmesan cheese
1 green onion (with top), finely chopped	2 green onions (with tops), finely chopped
1 tbsp margarine or butter, melted	2 tbsp margarine or butter, melted
¼ tsp browning sauce	½ tsp browning sauce
⅛ tsp salt	¼ tsp salt

Pound beef sirloin steak to ¼" thickness. Mix rice, cheese and onion[s]; spread over beef. Roll up; secure with string. Mix remaining ingredients; brush over beef roll[s]. Place on rack in 11 × 7 × 1½" dish. Cover with waxed paper and microwave on medium (275 watts) 3 min [5 min]; turn beef roll[s] over. Cover with waxed paper and microwave until beef is done, 1 to 3 min longer [3 to 5 min longer]. Remove string. Garnish with parsley sprigs and cherry tomato halves if desired.

Savory Minute Steak

1 Serving	[2 Servings]
1 beef cubed steak (3 to 4 oz)	2 beef cubed steaks (3 to 4 oz each)
⅛ tsp salt	¼ tsp salt
Dash of pepper	Dash of pepper
½ jar (2½-oz size) sliced mushrooms, drained	1 jar (2½-oz size) sliced mushrooms, drained
1 tbsp crumbled blue cheese	2 tbsp crumbled blue cheese
1 tbsp thinly sliced green onion (with top)	2 tbsp thinly sliced green onion (with top)
¼ tsp lemon juice	½ tsp lemon juice

Sprinkle both sides of beef cubed steak[s] with salt and pepper. Place beef in 8 × 8 × 2" dish; top with mushrooms. Cover with waxed paper and microwave on high (550 watts) until beef is tender and no longer pink, 2 to 2½ min [4 to 6 min]. Mix remaining ingredients; sprinkle over beef. Microwave uncovered until cheese is melted, about 30 sec [45 to 60 sec]. Garnish with green onions if desired.

Stuffed Beef Rolls, Glazed Carrots (page 92)

Oriental-style Beef and Vegetables

1 Serving	[2 Servings]
1/4 lb beef boneless sirloin steak	1/2 lb beef boneless sirloin steak
2 tbsp water	1/4 cup water
1 tbsp margarine or butter	2 tbsp margarine or butter
1 tsp sugar	2 tsp sugar
1/2 tsp instant beef bouillon	1 tsp instant beef bouillon
1/2 tsp cornstarch	1 tsp cornstarch
1 1/2 tsp soy sauce	1 tbsp soy sauce
2 green onions (with tops), cut into 1/2" pieces	4 green onions (with tops), cut into 1/2" pieces
1 small stalk celery, cut into 1/8" slices	2 small stalks celery, cut into 1/8" slices
1 cup bite-size pieces spinach	2 cups bite-size pieces spinach
4 mushrooms, thinly sliced	8 mushrooms, thinly sliced
3/4 cup hot cooked rice	1 1/2 cups hot cooked rice

For ease in cutting, freeze beef sirloin steak about 20 min. Cut beef across grain into 2 × 1/4" strips. Mix beef, water, margarine, sugar, bouillon (dry), cornstarch and soy sauce in 1-qt casserole [1 1/2-qt casserole]. Cover tightly and microwave on medium (275 watts), stirring twice, until beef is tender, 4 to 6 min [4 1/2 to 7 min]. Stir in onions and celery. Cover tightly and microwave on high (550 watts) until vegetables are crisp-tender, 1 1/2 to 2 min [2 to 3 min]. Stir in spinach and mushrooms. Cover tightly and microwave until spinach is cooked, 1 to 2 min [2 to 3 min]. Serve with rice.

Beef Burgundy

1 Serving	[2 Servings]
1/4 lb beef boneless round steak, cut into 1/2" pieces	1/2 lb beef boneless round steak, cut into 1/2" pieces
2 tsp all-purpose flour	1 tbsp plus 1 tsp all-purpose flour
2 tbsp dry red wine	1/4 cup dry red wine
2 tbsp water	1/4 cup water
1/4 tsp salt	1/2 tsp salt
1/4 tsp browning sauce	1/2 tsp browning sauce
Dash of pepper	Dash of pepper
Dash of ground thyme	Dash of ground thyme
1/8" slice medium onion, separated into rings	Two 1/8" slices medium onion, separated into rings
1/2 small clove garlic, finely chopped	1 small clove garlic, finely chopped
6 small mushrooms	12 small mushrooms

Coat beef round steak with flour in 21-oz casserole [1-qt casserole]. Stir in remaining ingredients except mushrooms. Cover tightly and microwave on medium-low (165 watts) 2 1/2 min [5 min]; stir. Cover tightly and microwave until beef and onion are tender, 2 1/2 to 6 1/2 min longer [5 to 7 min longer]. Stir in mushrooms. Cover tightly and microwave until mushrooms are tender, 1 1/2 to 2 min [3 to 5 min]. Garnish with parsley and serve with hard roll[s] if desired.

Beef Stroganoff

1 Serving	[2 Servings]
1/4 lb beef boneless sirloin steak (1/4" thick)	1/2 lb beef boneless sirloin steak (1/4" thick)
2 tbsp water	3 tbsp water
2 tsp margarine or butter	1 tbsp margarine or butter
1/2 tsp instant beef bouillon	1 tsp instant beef bouillon
1/2 tsp browning sauce	1 tsp browning sauce
Dash of pepper	1/8 tsp pepper
1/8" slice medium onion, separated into rings	Two 1/8" slices medium onion, separated into rings
1/2 small clove garlic, finely chopped	1 small clove garlic, finely chopped
2 mushrooms, sliced	4 mushrooms, sliced
1/4 cup dairy sour cream	1/2 cup dairy sour cream
Snipped parsley	Snipped parsley
3/4 cup hot cooked noodles	1 1/2 cups hot cooked noodles

For ease in cutting, freeze beef sirloin steak about 20 min. Cut beef across grain into 1 1/2 × 1/4" strips. Place beef, water, margarine, bouillon (dry), browning sauce, pepper, onion and garlic in 1-qt casserole [**1 1/2-qt casserole**]. Cover tightly and microwave on medium (275 watts), stirring twice, until beef is tender, 3 to 5 min [**4 to 7 min**]. Stir in mushrooms. Cover tightly and microwave 1 min [**1 1/4 to 1 1/2 min**]. Stir in sour cream thoroughly. Cover tightly and microwave just until hot, 15 to 20 sec [**45 to 60 sec**]. Sprinkle with parsley; serve over hot cooked noodles.

Petite Meat Loaf

1 Serving	[2 Servings]
1/4 lb ground beef	1/2 lb ground beef
3 tbsp soft bread crumbs	1/3 cup soft bread crumbs
2 tbsp milk	3 tbsp milk
1/2 tsp instant minced onion	1 tsp instant minced onion
1/2 tsp Worcestershire sauce	1 tsp Worcestershire sauce
1/8 tsp salt	1/4 tsp salt
1/8 tsp dry mustard	1/4 tsp dry mustard
Dash of pepper	Dash of pepper
Dash of ground sage	Dash of ground sage
Dash of garlic powder	Dash of garlic powder
1 tbsp barbecue sauce	2 tbsp barbecue sauce

Mix all ingredients except barbecue sauce. Spread in 10-oz casserole [**two 10-oz casseroles**]. Spread barbecue sauce over top[**s**]. Microwave uncovered on high (550 watts) until almost done, 2 to 3 min [**3 1/2 to 5 min**]. Let stand uncovered 3 min.

Salisbury-style Steak

1 Serving	[2 Servings]
1/4 lb ground beef	1/2 lb ground beef
1 tbsp dry bread crumbs	2 tbsp dry bread crumbs
1 tbsp milk	2 tbsp milk
1/8 tsp salt	1/4 tsp salt
Dash of pepper	1/8 tsp pepper
1/4 tsp browning sauce	1/2 tsp browning sauce
1/2 jar (2 1/2-oz size) sliced mushrooms, undrained	1 jar (2 1/2-oz) sliced mushrooms, undrained
1/2 tsp cornstarch	1 tsp cornstarch
1/4 tsp instant beef bouillon	1/2 tsp instant beef bouillon

Mix ground beef, bread crumbs, milk, salt and pepper. Shape into patty [**2 patties**], about 3/4" thick. Brush both sides with browning sauce. Place on rack in 11 × 7 × 1 1/2" dish. Cover with waxed paper and microwave on high (550 watts) until almost done, 2 to 3 1/4 min [**2 3/4 to 4 min**]. Mix mushrooms, cornstarch and bouillon (dry) in 1-cup measure. Microwave uncovered on high (550 watts), stirring once, until thickened, 45 to 60 sec [**1 3/4 to 2 min**]. Spoon over patty [**patties**].

Petite Meat Loaf, Broccoli with Swiss Cheese (page 90)

Garlic-Basil Burger

1 Serving	[2 Servings]
1/4 lb ground beef	1/2 lb ground beef
1 tbsp dry bread crumbs	2 tbsp dry bread crumbs
1 tbsp chopped green onion (with top)	2 tbsp chopped green onion (with top)
1/2 tsp lemon juice	1 tsp lemon juice
1/8 tsp salt	1/4 tsp salt
Dash of pepper	Dash of pepper
Dash of dried basil leaves	Dash of dried basil leaves
1/2 small clove garlic, finely chopped	1 small clove garlic, finely chopped
1 slice bacon	2 slices bacon

Mix all ingredients except bacon. Shape into patty [2 patties], about 3/4" thick. Place on rack in 11 × 7 × 1½" dish. Cover with waxed paper and microwave on high (550 watts) until almost done, 2 to 3¼ min [2¾ to 4 min]. Remove from rack; let stand 3 min.

Place bacon on rack in same dish. Cover loosely and microwave on high (550 watts) until nearly crisp, 1¼ to 1½ min [1½ to 2½ min]; drain. Crisscross half slices of bacon on patty [patties]. Garnish with pickles if desired.

Meatballs

1 Serving	[2 Servings]
1/4 lb ground beef	1/2 lb ground beef
1 tbsp dry bread crumbs	2 tbsp dry bread crumbs
1 tbsp finely chopped onion	2 tbsp finely chopped onion
2 tbsp milk	3 tbsp milk
1/4 tsp Worcestershire sauce	1/2 tsp Worcestershire sauce
1/8 tsp salt	1/4 tsp salt
Dash of pepper	Dash of pepper
Dash of garlic powder	Dash of garlic powder

Mix all ingredients; shape into 1½-inch balls. Place meatballs in 21-oz casserole [9 × 1¼" pie plate]. Cover loosely and microwave on high (550 watts) 1 min; turn meatballs over. Cover loosely and microwave until inside is no longer pink, 30 sec to 2 min [1½ to 3 min]. Let stand loosely covered 3 min; drain. Serve with hot commercially prepared spaghetti sauce if desired.

Garlic-Basil Burger

Meatballs in Wine Sauce

1 Serving	[2 Servings]
Meatballs (page 20)	Meatballs (page 20)
1/3 cup water	2/3 cup water
1 tsp cornstarch	2 tsp cornstarch
1 tbsp dry red wine	2 tbsp dry red wine
1/2 tsp soy sauce	1 tsp soy sauce
1/4 tsp instant beef bouillon	1/2 tsp instant beef bouillon
1/8 tsp salt	1/4 tsp salt
Dash of pepper	Dash of pepper
3/4 cup hot cooked rice	1 1/2 cups hot cooked rice

Prepare Meatballs; keep warm. Mix water and cornstarch in 1-cup measure [2-cup measure]; gradually stir in wine, soy sauce, bouillon (dry), the salt and pepper. Microwave uncovered on high (550 watts), stirring every min, until boiling, 1 1/2 to 2 min [1 1/2 to 2 1/2 min]. Pour over meatballs; stir gently. Serve over hot rice sprinkled with snipped parsley if desired.

Chili con Carne

1 Serving	[2 Servings]
1/4 lb ground beef	1/2 lb ground beef
2 tbsp finely chopped onion	1/4 cup finely chopped onion
1 tsp chili powder	2 tsp chili powder
1/8 tsp salt	1/4 tsp salt
Dash of ground red pepper	Dash of ground red pepper
1/2 small clove garlic, finely chopped	1 small clove garlic, finely chopped
1 can (7 1/2 oz) whole tomatoes, undrained	1 can (14 1/2 oz) whole tomatoes, undrained
1/2 can (8-oz size) kidney beans, undrained	1 can (8 oz) kidney beans, undrained

Crumble ground beef into 16-oz casserole [1-qt casserole]. Cover loosely and microwave on high (550 watts) until very little pink remains, 1 to 1 1/2 min [1 1/2 to 2 min]; break up and drain. Stir in remaining ingredients except beans; break up tomatoes. Cover loosely and microwave until onion is cooked, 2 to 3 min [4 to 5 min]. Stir in beans. Cover loosely and microwave until hot, 1 1/2 to 2 min [2 1/2 to 3 min]. Sprinkle with shredded Cheddar cheese and chopped green onions if desired.

Meatballs in Wine Sauce

Beef Tacos

1 Serving	[2 Servings]
¼ lb ground beef	½ lb ground beef
2 tbsp chopped onion	¼ cup chopped onion
½ tsp finely chopped green chilies	1 tsp finely chopped green chilies
⅛ tsp salt	¼ tsp salt
Dash of ground cumin	Dash of ground cumin
½ small clove garlic, finely chopped	1 small clove garlic, finely chopped
¼ cup chopped avocado	½ cup chopped avocado
1 tsp lemon juice	2 tsp lemon juice
¼ cup chopped tomato	½ cup chopped tomato
2 taco shells	4 taco shells
Dairy sour cream	Dairy sour cream
Shredded Cheddar cheese	Shredded Cheddar cheese

Crumble ground beef into 2-cup measure [**4-cup measure**]. Cover loosely and microwave on high (550 watts) until very little pink remains, 1 to 1¼ min [**1½ to 2 min**]; break up and drain. Stir in onion, chilies, salt, cumin and garlic. Microwave uncovered until hot and onion is cooked, 1 to 2 min [**2 to 3 min**].

Toss avocado and lemon juice; stir avocado and tomato into beef mixture. Spoon into taco shells. Top with sour cream and cheese. Serve with taco sauce if desired.

Spicy Ground Beef and Zucchini

1 Serving	[2 Servings]
¼ lb ground beef	½ lb ground beef
½ cup ¼" slices zucchini	1 cup ¼" slices zucchini
⅛" slice medium onion, separated into rings	Two ⅛" slices medium onion, separated into rings
¼ cup chili sauce	½ cup chili sauce
2 tbsp chopped green pepper	¼ cup chopped green pepper
1 tsp brown sugar	2 tsp brown sugar
¼ tsp chili powder	½ tsp chili powder
⅛ tsp salt	¼ tsp salt
Dash of pepper	Dash of pepper
1 tsp grated Parmesan cheese	2 tsp grated Parmesan cheese

Crumble ground beef into 16-oz casserole [**1-qt casserole**]. Cover loosely and microwave on high (550 watts) until very little pink remains, 1 to 1¼ min [**1½ to 2 min**]; break up and drain. Stir in zucchini and onion. Mix chili sauce, green pepper, brown sugar, chili powder, salt and pepper; spread over beef mixture. Cover loosely and microwave until vegetables are crisp-tender, 1½ to 2 min [**3 to 4 min**]. Sprinkle with cheese.

Beef Tacos

Beef-stuffed Romaine Leaves

1 Serving	[2 Servings]
2 large romaine leaves	4 large romaine leaves
1/4 lb ground beef	1/2 lb ground beef
2 tbsp uncooked instant rice	1/4 cup uncooked instant rice
1 tbsp finely chopped onion	2 tbsp finely chopped onion
1 tbsp tomato sauce	2 tbsp tomato sauce
1 tsp prepared horseradish	2 tsp prepared horseradish
1/8 tsp salt	1/4 tsp salt
1/4 cup tomato sauce	1/2 cup tomato sauce
1 tsp snipped parsley	2 tsp snipped parsley
Dash of red pepper sauce	Dash of red pepper sauce

Cover romaine leaves with boiling water. Let stand until pliable, 3 to 4 min; drain. Mix ground beef, rice, onion, 1 tbsp [2 tbsp] tomato sauce, the horseradish and salt. Place 1/2 [1/4] of the beef mixture at stem end of each leaf; roll leaf around beef mixture, tucking in sides.

Place romaine rolls, seam sides down, in 21-oz casserole [9 × 1 1/4" pie plate]. Mix remaining ingredients; pour over romaine rolls. Cover loosely and microwave on high (550 watts) until beef is partially done, 2 to 3 min; rotate casserole [pie plate] 1/2 turn. Spoon sauce over romaine rolls. Cover loosely and microwave until beef is done, 1 1/2 to 3 min longer [3 to 5 min longer]. Let stand loosely covered 1 min.

Beef-stuffed Romaine Leaves

25

Spaghetti with Meat Sauce

1 Serving	[2 Servings]
¼ lb ground beef	½ **lb ground beef**
½ cup tomato sauce	1 **cup tomato sauce**
2 tbsp dry red wine	3 **tbsp dry red wine**
1 tbsp chopped onion	2 **tbsp chopped onion**
1 tbsp finely chopped green pepper	2 **tbsp finely chopped green pepper**
⅛ tsp salt	¼ **tsp salt**
Dash of pepper	**Dash of pepper**
Dash of dried basil leaves	**Dash of dried basil leaves**
1 small clove garlic, crushed	1 **large clove garlic, crushed**
2 mushrooms, thinly sliced	4 **mushrooms, thinly sliced**
1 cup hot cooked spaghetti	2 **cups hot cooked spaghetti**

Crumble ground beef into 2-cup measure [**4-cup measure**]. Cover loosely and microwave on high (550 watts) until very little pink remains, 1 to 1¼ min [**1½ to 2 min**]; break up and drain. Stir in remaining ingredients except spaghetti. Cover loosely and microwave 1 min [**2 min**]; stir. Cover loosely and microwave until bubbly and mushrooms are tender, 1½ to 2 min [**1½ to 2 min**]. Pour over hot spaghetti. Serve with grated Parmesan cheese if desired.

Stuffed Onion

1 Serving	[2 Servings]
1 medium Bermuda onion, peeled	2 **medium Bermuda onions, peeled**
¼ lb ground beef	½ **lb ground beef**
⅓ cup tomato sauce	⅔ **cup tomato sauce**
⅛ tsp salt	¼ **tsp salt**
⅛ tsp dried oregano leaves	¼ **tsp dried oregano leaves**
6 drops red pepper sauce	12 **drops red pepper sauce**
½ small clove garlic, finely chopped	1 **small clove garlic, finely chopped**
1 tbsp shredded mozzarella cheese	2 **tbsp shredded mozzarella cheese**

Place onion[s] in 16-oz casserole [**two 16-oz casseroles**]. Cover with waxed paper and microwave on high (550 watts) 2 min [**3½ min**]; turn onion[s] over. Cover and microwave until tender, 2 to 3 min longer [**3½ to 4½ min longer**]. Scoop out onion[s], leaving ½" wall[s]. Reserve shell[s]. Chop center[s] of onion[s]; reserve.

Crumble ground beef into 16-oz casserole. Cover loosely and microwave on high (550 watts) until very little pink remains, 1 to 1¼ min [**1½ to 2 min**]; break up and drain. Stir in chopped onion, tomato sauce, salt, oregano, pepper sauce and garlic.

Place onion[s] in 16-oz casserole [**two 16-oz casseroles**]; fill with beef mixture. Microwave uncovered on high (550 watts) until beef mixture and onion[s] are hot, 2 to 3 min [**3 to 4 min**]. Sprinkle with cheese.

Liver-Bacon Rolls

1 Serving	[2 Servings]
1 slice bacon, cut into ½" pieces	2 slices bacon, cut into ½" pieces
2 pieces (1½ oz each) beef liver (¼" thick)	4 pieces (1½ oz each) beef liver (¼" thick)
2 green onions (with tops), about 6" long	4 green onions (with tops), about 6" long
2 tbsp finely chopped green pepper	¼ cup finely chopped green pepper
½ can (8-oz size) stewed tomatoes	1 can (8 oz) stewed tomatoes
4 drops red pepper sauce	8 drops red pepper sauce
¾ cup hot cooked rice	1½ cups hot cooked rice

Place bacon in 1-qt casserole. Cover loosely and microwave on high (550 watts) until almost crisp, 1¼ to 2 min [**2 to 2¼ min**]; drain and reserve. Wrap 1 piece liver around 1 onion; secure with wooden picks. Repeat with remaining liver and onion[**s**]. Place liver rolls in casserole. Top with green pepper. Mix tomatoes, pepper sauce and bacon; pour over liver. Cover loosely and microwave on medium-high (385 watts) 3 min [**4 min**]; turn liver over. Cover loosely and microwave until done, 2 to 4 min longer [**3 to 5 min longer**]. Remove wooden picks. Spoon sauce over liver; serve with rice.

Ham Slice with Rum Marmalade

1 Serving	[2 Servings]
1 slice (3 oz) fully cooked smoked ham (¼" thick)	2 slices (3 oz each) fully cooked smoked ham (¼" thick)
2 tbsp orange marmalade	¼ cup orange marmalade
1 tbsp rum	2 tbsp rum
½ tsp cornstarch	1 tsp cornstarch
Dash of ground nutmeg	⅛ tsp ground nutmeg

Place ham on rack in 11 × 7 × 1½" dish. Mix remaining ingredients; spoon over ham. Cover with waxed paper and microwave on medium-high (385 watts) until hot, 2 to 3 min [**3 to 4 min**]. Garnish ham slice[**s**] with ¼ orange slice if desired.

Liver-Bacon Rolls

Ham Rolls with Corn

1 Serving	[2 Servings]

2 thin slices (1 oz each) fully cooked smoked ham, each 6 × 4"
1 tbsp cream cheese, softened
2 small green onions (with tops), each 8" long
½ can (8-oz size) cream-style corn
1 tbsp chopped green pepper
1 tsp margarine or butter, softened

4 thin slices (1 oz each) fully cooked smoked ham, each 6 × 4"
2 tbsp cream cheese, softened
4 small green onions (with tops), each 8" long
1 can (8 oz) cream-style corn
2 tbsp chopped green pepper
2 tsp margarine or butter, softened

Spread ham with cream cheese. Cut onions crosswise into halves. Place 2 halves on each ham slice; roll up. Mix corn, green pepper and margarine; pour into 14-oz shallow casserole [**two 14-oz shallow casseroles**]. Top with ham rolls, seam sides down. Cover tightly and microwave on high (550 watts) until corn is hot, 1 to 2 min [**3 to 4 min**].

Hot Ham Salad

1 Serving	[2 Servings]

2 slices (1 oz each) sliced chopped ham, cut into ½" pieces
¼ cup herb seasoned croutons
¼ cup thinly sliced celery
¼ cup frozen green peas, thawed
¼ cup salad dressing
¼ tsp instant minced onion
Dash of pepper
1 tbsp shredded Cheddar cheese

4 slices (1 oz each) sliced chopped ham, cut into ½" pieces
½ cup herb seasoned croutons
½ cup thinly sliced celery
½ cup frozen green peas, thawed
½ cup salad dressing
½ tsp instant minced onion
⅛ tsp pepper
2 tbsp shredded Cheddar cheese

Mix all ingredients except cheese. Spoon lightly into 14-oz shallow casserole [**two 14-oz shallow casseroles**]. Sprinkle with cheese. Cover loosely and microwave on medium-high (385 watts) until hot and bubbly, 2½ to 3½ min [**3½ to 4½ min**].

Ham Rolls with Corn

Pork with Cranberry Chutney Sauce

1 Serving	[2 Servings]
3-oz slice fully cooked pork (¼" thick)	Two 3-oz slices fully cooked pork (¼" thick)
1 tsp margarine or butter, melted	2 tsp margarine or butter, melted
2 tbsp whole berry cranberry sauce	¼ cup whole berry cranberry sauce
1 tbsp finely chopped green onion (with top)	2 tbsp finely chopped green onion (with top)
1 tbsp finely chopped green pepper	2 tbsp finely chopped green pepper
½ tsp tarragon vinegar	1 tsp tarragon vinegar
Dash of salt	⅛ tsp salt
Dash of allspice	⅛ tsp allspice

Place pork slice[s] in 12-oz shallow casserole [22-oz shallow casserole]. Brush with margarine. Mix remaining ingredients; spoon over pork. Cover with waxed paper and microwave on medium-high (385 watts) 1 min [2 min]; rotate casserole ½ turn. Microwave until hot, 1½ to 2½ min longer [2 to 3 min longer]. Serve with corn sticks if desired.

Pork and Rice

1 Serving	[2 Servings]
¼ cup ¼" thick diagonal slices carrots	½ cup ¼" thick diagonal slices carrots
1 tsp margarine or butter	2 tsp margarine or butter
½ cup ½" pieces cooked pork	1 cup ½" pieces cooked pork
¼ cup uncooked instant rice	½ cup uncooked instant rice
¼ cup hot water	½ cup hot water
2 tsp soy sauce	1 tbsp plus 1 tsp soy sauce
¼ tsp instant chicken bouillon	½ tsp instant chicken bouillon
⅛ tsp ground ginger	¼ tsp ground ginger
3 medium mushrooms, thinly sliced	6 medium mushrooms, thinly sliced
1 green onion (with top), finely chopped	2 green onions (with tops), finely chopped

Place carrots and margarine in 15-oz casserole [24-oz casserole]. Cover with vented plastic wrap and microwave on high (550 watts) until carrots are crisp-tender, 1 to 2 min [2 to 3 min]. Stir in pork, rice, water, soy sauce, bouillon (dry) and ginger. Cover and microwave 1 min [2 min]; stir. Cover and microwave until liquid is absorbed, 1 to 2 min longer [2 to 3 min longer]. Stir in mushrooms and onion[s]. Cover and microwave 1 min [2 min].

29

Lemon-Honey Pork Chop

1 Serving	[2 Servings]
4-oz pork loin chop (1/2" thick)	Two 4-oz pork loin chops (1/2" thick)
1/8 tsp salt	1/4 tsp salt
Dash of pepper	1/8 tsp pepper
1 tbsp water	2 tbsp water
1 tbsp honey	2 tbsp honey
1/8 tsp grated lemon peel	1/4 tsp grated lemon peel
1 1/2 tsp lemon juice	1 tbsp lemon juice
1/4 tsp parsley flakes	1/2 tsp parsley flakes
1/2 small clove garlic, finely chopped	1 small clove garlic, finely chopped
1/2 tsp cornstarch	1 tsp cornstarch
1 1/2 tsp cold water	1 tbsp cold water
1 thin slice lemon	2 thin slices lemon

Place pork chop[s] in 22-oz shallow casserole [8 × 8 × 2" dish, with narrow ends toward center]. Sprinkle with salt and pepper. Mix 1 tbsp [2 tbsp] water, the honey, lemon peel, lemon juice, parsley and garlic; pour over pork. Cover tightly and microwave on medium (275 watts) 3 min [5 min]; rotate casserole [dish] 1/4 turn. Microwave until pork is done, 4 to 7 min [12 to 15 min], rotating casserole 1/4 turn every 3 min. Meat thermometer should register 170° when inserted in pork in several places.

Mix cornstarch and 1 1/2 tsp [1 tbsp] water; stir into mixture in casserole [dish]. Cover and microwave until mixture thickens and boils, 30 to 60 sec [1 to 2 min]. Spoon sauce over pork. Garnish with lemon slice[s]. Serve with hot cooked rice if desired.

Pork Tenderloin with Mustard Sauce

1 Serving	[2 Servings]
1 piece pork tenderloin (4 oz)	2 pieces pork tenderloin (4 oz each)
1/8 tsp salt	1/4 tsp salt
2 tbsp chopped onion	1/4 cup chopped onion
2 tbsp chopped green pepper	1/4 cup chopped green pepper
2 tbsp water	1/4 cup water
2 tsp Dijon-style mustard	1 tbsp plus 1 tsp Dijon-style mustard
1/2 tsp all-purpose flour	1 tsp all-purpose flour

Place pork tenderloin in 16-oz shallow casserole [24-oz shallow casserole]. Sprinkle with salt and

onion. Cover tightly and microwave on medium (275 watts) 2 min [4 min]; rotate casserole 1/4 turn. Microwave 2 min longer [4 min longer]. Mix remaining ingredients; spoon over pork. Cover tightly and microwave, rotating casserole 1/4 turn every 3 min, until pork is done, 2 to 4 min [4 to 6 min]. Meat thermometer should register 170° when inserted in pork in several places.

Pork and Rice Curry

1 Serving	[2 Servings]
1/2 slice bacon, finely chopped	1 slice bacon, finely chopped
Two 1/8" slices onion, separated into rings	Four 1/8" slices onion, separated into rings
1/2 cup 1/2" pieces fully cooked pork	1 cup 1/2" pieces fully cooked pork
1/4 cup uncooked instant rice	1/2 cup uncooked instant rice
1/4 cup hot water	1/2 cup hot water
1 tbsp raisins	2 tbsp raisins
1/2 tsp instant chicken bouillon	1 tsp instant chicken bouillon
1/2 tsp curry powder	1 tsp curry powder
Dash of ground cinnamon	1/8 tsp ground cinnamon
Chopped peanuts	Chopped peanuts
Chopped tomatoes	Chopped tomatoes

Place bacon and onion in 12-oz casserole [22-oz casserole]. Cover with vented plastic wrap and microwave on high (550 watts) until onion is tender, 1 to 2 min [2 to 3 min]. Stir in remaining ingredients except peanuts and tomatoes. Cover with vented plastic wrap and microwave 1 min [2 min]; stir. Cover with vented plastic wrap and microwave until water is absorbed, 1 to 2 min [2 to 3 min]. Sprinkle with peanuts and tomatoes.

Currant-glazed Pork Chop

1 Serving	[2 Servings]
2 tbsp red currant jelly	¼ cup red currant jelly
2 tbsp chili sauce	¼ cup chili sauce
Dash of ground allspice	⅛ tsp ground allspice
1 smoked pork chop, ½" thick	2 smoked pork chops, ½" thick

Mix jelly, chili sauce and allspice in 1-cup measure. Cover with waxed paper and microwave on high (550 watts) until melted, 30 to 45 sec [1 to 1½ min].

Trim excess fat from pork chop[s]. Place pork in 16-oz shallow casserole [8 × 8 × 2" dish, with narrow ends toward center]. Spread half of the jelly mixture over pork. Cover tightly and microwave on high (550 watts) 1 min [2 min]. Turn pork over and spread with remaining jelly mixture; rotate casserole [dish] ¼ turn. Cover and microwave until pork is done, 2½ to 3½ min [4 to 6 min]. Meat thermometer should register 160° when inserted in pork in several places.

Sweet-and-Sour Pork

1 Serving	[2 Servings]
3 oz pork tenderloin, cut into ½" pieces	6 oz pork tenderloin, cut into ½" pieces
1 tsp margarine or butter	2 tsp margarine or butter
½ can (8¼-oz size) pineapple chunks in syrup, drained (reserve ¼ cup syrup)	1 can (8¼ oz) pineapple chunks in syrup, drained (reserve ½ cup syrup)
1 tsp cornstarch	2 tsp cornstarch
2 tbsp catsup	¼ cup catsup
1 tsp sugar	2 tsp sugar
1 tsp soy sauce	2 tsp soy sauce
4 drops red pepper sauce	⅛ tsp red pepper sauce
¼ medium green pepper, cut into ⅛" strips	½ medium green pepper, cut into ⅛" strips
3 cherry tomatoes, cut into halves	6 cherry tomatoes, cut into halves
¾ cup hot cooked rice	1½ cups hot cooked rice

Mix pork and margarine in 15-oz casserole [1-qt casserole]. Cover tightly and microwave on medium (275 watts), stirring every 2 min, until pork is no longer pink, 2 to 3 min [4 to 6 min]. Add enough water to reserved pineapple syrup to measure ⅓ cup [⅔ cup]; stir in cornstarch. Stir syrup mixture, catsup, sugar, soy sauce and pepper sauce into pork mixture. Cover tightly and microwave, stirring every 2 min, until mixture thickens and boils and pork is tender, 4 to 5 min [6 to 8 min]. Cut pineapple chunks into halves. Stir pineapple, green pepper and tomatoes into pork mixture. Cover and microwave until hot, 1 to 2 min [2 to 3 min]. Serve over hot rice.

Currant-Glazed Pork Chop

Pork and Chinese Pea Pods

1 Serving	[2 Servings]
3 oz pork tenderloin, cut into ½" pieces (⅓ cup)	6 oz pork tenderloin, cut into ½" pieces (⅔ cup)
1 tbsp margarine or butter	2 tbsp margarine or butter
⅓ cup water	⅔ cup water
1½ tsp cornstarch	1 tbsp cornstarch
½ tsp instant chicken bouillon	1 tsp instant chicken bouillon
1½ tsp soy sauce	1 tbsp soy sauce
1½ tsp Dijon-style mustard	1 tbsp Dijon-style mustard
⅛ tsp ground ginger	¼ tsp ground ginger
½ small clove garlic, crushed	1 small clove garlic, crushed
¼ cup frozen small whole onions	½ cup frozen small whole onions
½ cup Chinese pea pods (about 15)	1 cup Chinese pea pods (about 30)
½ small tomato, cut into 6 wedges	1 small tomato, cut into 6 wedges
¾ cup hot cooked rice	1½ cups hot cooked rice

Mix pork and margarine in 15-oz casserole [**1-qt casserole**]. Cover tightly and microwave on medium (275 watts), stirring every 3 min, until pork is no longer pink, 3 to 5 min [**6 to 9 min**]. Mix water, cornstarch, bouillon (dry), soy sauce, mustard, ginger and garlic; stir into pork mixture. Stir in onions. Cover tightly and microwave, stirring every 3 min, until mixture boils and pork is tender, 4 to 6 min [**9 to 12 min**]. Stir in pea pods. Cover tightly and microwave on high (550 watts) until pea pods are crisp-tender, 1 to 3 min [**2 to 4 min**]. Stir in tomato. Serve over hot rice.

Pork and Chinese Pea Pods

Fruited Pork

1 Serving	[2 Servings]
4 oz pork boneless shoulder, cut into 1/2" pieces (1/2 cup)	8 oz pork boneless shoulder, cut into 1/2" pieces (1 cup)
2 tbsp chopped onion	1/4 cup chopped onion
1/4 cup chopped apple	1/2 cup chopped apple
2 tbsp water	1/4 cup water
1 tsp all-purpose flour	2 tsp all-purpose flour
1/2 tsp instant chicken bouillon	1 tsp instant chicken bouillon
Dash of salt	1/8 tsp salt
1/2 can (8-oz size) sauerkraut, drained	1 can (8 oz) sauerkraut, drained
4 dried apricots or prunes, cut up	8 dried apricots or prunes, cut up
3/4 cup hot cooked spaetzle or noodles	1 1/2 cups hot cooked spaetzle or noodles
Snipped parsley	Snipped parsley

Mix pork and onion in 15-oz casserole [**1-qt casserole**]. Cover tightly and microwave on medium (275 watts), stirring every 3 min, until pork is tender, 5 to 7 min [**9 to 12 min**]. Stir in remaining ingredients except spaetzle and parsley. Cover and microwave, stirring every 3 min, until hot and thickened, 3 to 4 min [**5 to 7 min**]. Serve over hot spaetzle and sprinkle with parsley.

Pork Chow Mein

1 Serving	[2 Servings]
4 oz coarsely ground pork (1/2 cup)	8 oz coarsely ground pork (1 cup)
1/4 cup water	1/2 cup water
1 tsp cornstarch	2 tsp cornstarch
2 tsp soy sauce	1 tbsp plus 1 tsp soy sauce
1/2 tsp sugar	1 tsp sugar
1/2 tsp browning sauce	1 tsp browning sauce
Dash of garlic powder	1/8 tsp garlic powder
1 cup bean sprouts	2 cups bean sprouts
1/4 cup 1/8" thick diagonal slices celery	1/2 cup 1/8" thick diagonal slices celery
2 green onions (with tops), cut into 1/2" pieces	4 green onions (with tops), cut into 1/2" pieces
3/4 cup chow mein noodles	1 1/2 cups chow mein noodles

Mix pork, water, cornstarch, soy sauce, sugar, browning sauce and garlic powder in 15-oz casserole [**1-qt casserole**]. Cover tightly and microwave on high (550 watts), stirring every 2 min, until mixture thickens and boils and pork is no longer pink, 3 to 5 min [**5 to 8 min**]. Stir in bean sprouts, celery and onions. Cover tightly and microwave until vegetables are crisp-tender, 2 to 3 min [**4 to 5 min**]. Serve over chow mein noodles.

Fruited Pork

Salami Tortilla

1 Serving	[2 Servings]
Two 6" corn tortillas, cut into halves	Four 6" corn tortillas, cut into halves
1/4 cup jalapeño bean dip	1/2 cup jalapeño bean dip
2 oz sliced Genoa salami (about 8 slices)	4 oz sliced Genoa salami (about 16 slices)
4 tsp salsa	8 tsp salsa
2 thin slices tomato	4 thin slices tomato
2 tbsp shredded Cheddar cheese	1/4 cup shredded Cheddar cheese

Spread tortilla halves with bean dip. Place 1 tortilla half in 22-oz casserole [**2 tortilla halves in 8 × 8 × 2" dish**]; top tortilla half [**each tortilla half**] with 2 slices salami and 1 tsp salsa. Repeat layers 3 times. Cover with waxed paper and microwave on high (550 watts) until hot, 2 to 3 min [**3 to 4 min**]. Top wth tomatoes and cheese. Microwave uncovered until cheese is melted, 30 sec to 1½ min [**1 to 1½ min**]. Serve with dairy sour cream and additional salsa if desired.

Sausage-filled Tortilla

1 Serving	[2 Servings]
1/8 lb bulk pork sausage	1/4 lb bulk pork sausage
2 tbsp coarsely chopped tomato	1/4 cup coarsely chopped tomato
1 tsp chili powder	2 tsp chili powder
1 tsp lemon juice	2 tsp lemon juice
Dash of salt	1/8 tsp salt
1/2 small clove garlic, finely chopped	1 small clove garlic, finely chopped
Two 6" flour tortillas	Four 6" flour tortillas
1/4 cup refried beans	1/2 cup refried beans
1/4 cup shredded Cheddar cheese	1/2 cup shredded Cheddar cheese
Vegetable oil	Vegetable oil
2 tbsp salsa	1/4 cup salsa

Crumble pork sausage into 6 × 4 × 1½" dish [**8 × 8 × 2" dish**]. Cover with waxed paper and microwave on high (550 watts) until very little pink remains, 30 to 60 sec [**1¼ to 1½ min**]; break up and drain. Stir in tomato, chili powder, lemon juice, salt and garlic. Cover tightly and microwave until hot, 30 to 60 sec [**1½ to 2 min**]; stir.

Wrap tortillas in very damp cloth and microwave on high (550 watts) until softened, 30 to 45 sec [**45 to 60 sec**]. Spread 2 tbsp refried beans over each tortilla. Spoon 2 tbsp sausage mixture onto center; sprinkle with 2 tbsp cheese. Roll up. Arrange tortillas, seams sides down, in dish. Brush tops with oil. Cover tightly and microwave until hot, 1½ to 2 min [**2½ to 3 min**]. Spoon salsa over tortillas.

Sausage-Vegetable Kabobs

1 Serving	[2 Servings]
3 oz fully cooked kielbasa, cut into 4 pieces	**6 oz fully cooked kielbasa, cut into 8 pieces**
1 small whole onion, cut into fourths	**2 small whole onions, cut into fourths**
2 medium mushrooms	**4 medium mushrooms**
Four ½" pieces zucchini	**Eight ½" pieces zucchini**
2 tbsp taco sauce	**¼ cup taco sauce**
1 tsp vegetable oil	**2 tsp vegetable oil**
2 cherry tomatoes	**4 cherry tomatoes**

Alternate kielbasa, onion pieces, mushrooms and zucchini on 2 wooden skewers [**4 wooden skewers**], placing onion pieces on ends and mushrooms in centers. Mix taco sauce and oil; brush over kabobs. Place on 10" plate. Cover with waxed paper and microwave on high (550 watts) 1¼ min [**2 min**]; rearrange kabobs. Cover with waxed paper and microwave until hot, 1¼ to 2¼ min longer [**2 to 3 min longer**]. Place cherry tomatoes on ends of skewers. Cover with waxed paper and microwave until warm, 30 to 45 sec [**45 to 60 sec**]. Serve with rice if desired.

Frank and Rice Stew

1 Serving	[2 Servings]
2 frankfurters (1½ oz each), cut diagonally into ½" pieces	**4 frankfurters (1½ oz each), cut diagonally into ½" pieces**
⅓ cup uncooked instant rice	**⅔ cup uncooked instant rice**
⅛ tsp salt	**¼ tsp salt**
⅛ tsp dried basil leaves	**¼ tsp dried basil leaves**
Dash of pepper	**⅛ tsp pepper**
1 can (7½ oz) whole tomatoes, undrained	**1 can (14½ oz) whole tomatoes, undrained**
1 can (2 oz) mushroom stems and pieces, undrained	**1 can (4 oz) mushroom stems and pieces, undrained**
1 green onion, finely chopped	**2 green onions, finely chopped**

Mix all ingredients except onion[**s**] in 16 oz casserole [**1-qt casserole**]. Cover tightly and microwave on high (550 watts) 1½ to 2 min [**2½ to 3 min**]; stir. Cover tightly and microwave until rice is tender and water is absorbed, 1½ to 2 min longer [**2½ to 3 min longer**]. Sprinkle with onion[**s**]. Cover tightly and let stand 5 min.

Curried Lamb

1 Serving	[2 Servings]
1 tbsp margarine or butter	2 tbsp margarine or butter
1 tbsp chopped onion	2 tbsp chopped onion
1 tbsp all-purpose flour	2 tbsp all-purpose flour
1/3 cup water	2/3 cup water
1/2 tsp instant chicken bouillon	1 tsp instant chicken bouillon
1/2 tsp curry powder	1 tsp curry powder
1/4 tsp salt	1/2 tsp salt
3 oz cooked lamb, cut into 1/2" pieces (1/2 cup)	6 oz cooked lamb, cut into 1/2" pieces (1 cup)
1 tbsp chopped green pepper	2 tbsp chopped green pepper
2 tbsp dairy sour cream	1/4 cup dairy sour cream
3/4 cup hot cooked rice	1 1/2 cups hot cooked rice

Place margarine and onion in 22-oz casserole [**1-qt casserole**]. Microwave uncovered on high (550 watts) until onion is crisp-tender, 45 to 60 sec [**1 1/4 to 1 1/2 min**]. Mix in flour. Stir in water, bouillon (dry), curry powder and salt. Microwave uncovered 30 sec [**60 sec**]; stir. Microwave uncovered until thickened, 15 to 30 sec longer [**30 to 60 sec longer**]. Stir in lamb and green pepper. Cover tightly and microwave until hot, 2 to 3 min [**3 to 4 min**]. Stir in sour cream. Cover tightly and let stand 3 min. Serve over rice. Garnish with finely chopped apple and serve with chutney if desired.

Lamb Loaf with Kiwifruit-Mint Sauce

1 Serving	[2 Servings]
Kiwifruit-Mint Sauce (below)	Kiwifruit-Mint Sauce (below)
1/4 lb ground lamb	1/2 lb ground lamb
3 tbsp soft bread crumbs	1/3 cup soft bread crumbs
2 tbsp dry red wine	1/4 cup dry red wine
1/8 tsp salt	1/4 tsp salt
Dash of dried rosemary leaves, crushed	1/8 tsp dried rosemary leaves, crushed
1/2 small clove garlic, finely chopped	1 small clove garlic, finely chopped

Prepare Kiwifruit-Mint Sauce. Mix remaining ingredients. Shape into 4×2" loaf [**6×3" loaf**] in greased shallow 10-oz casserole [**9×1 1/4" pie plate**]. Microwave uncovered on high (550 watts) 2 min; rotate casserole [**pie plate**] 1/4 turn. Microwave uncovered until almost done, 1 to 2 min [**2 to 3 min**]. Let stand uncovered 3 min. Serve with Kiwifruit-Mint Sauce. Garnish with mint leaves and kiwifruit if desired.

Kiwifruit-Mint Sauce

1/4 kiwifruit, pared and mashed (1 tbsp)	1/2 kiwifruit, pared and mashed (2 tbsp)
1 tsp snipped fresh mint leaves or 1/8 tsp dried mint leaves, crushed	2 tsp snipped fresh mint leaves or 1/4 tsp dried mint leaves, crushed
1/2 tsp sugar	1 tsp sugar
1/2 tsp lime juice	1 tsp lime juice

Mix all ingredients.

Saucy Veal Cutlet

Hungarian-style Veal

1 Serving	[2 Servings]
1 tbsp margarine or butter	2 tbsp margarine or butter
1 tbsp finely chopped onion	2 tbsp finely chopped onion
1 tsp instant chicken bouillon	2 tsp instant chicken bouillon
1/4 lb veal boneless round steak (1/2" thick), cut into 3 × 1/2" strips	1/2 lb veal boneless round steak (1/2" thick), cut into 3 × 1/2" strips
1 tbsp all-purpose flour	2 tbsp all-purpose flour
1/2 tsp paprika	1 tsp paprika
Dash of salt	1/8 tsp salt
Dash of pepper	Dash of pepper
1/3 cup half-and-half	2/3 cup half-and-half
2 tbsp dairy sour cream	1/4 cup dairy sour cream
3/4 cup hot cooked noodles	1 1/2 cups hot cooked noodles

Place margarine, onion and bouillon (dry) in 22-oz casserole [**1-qt casserole**]. Microwave uncovered on high (550 watts) until margarine is melted, about 45 sec [**about 1½ min**]. Place veal round steak in casserole, turning to coat with margarine mixture. Cover tightly and microwave on medium (275 watts) 3 min [**4½ min**]; stir. Cover tightly and microwave until veal is done, 2 to 3 min longer [**3½ to 4½ min longer**].

Remove veal from casserole; reserve. Mix flour, paprika, salt and pepper into mixture in casserole. Stir in half-and-half. Microwave uncovered on medium-high (385 watts), stirring twice, until thickened, 1¼ to 2½ min [**2¼ to 4 min**]. Mix in sour cream. Stir in veal. Cover loosely and microwave on medium (275 watts) until hot, 1½ to 2 min [**3 to 4 min**]. Serve over hot noodles. Sprinkle with paprika if desired.

Saucy Veal Cutlet

1 Serving	[2 Servings]
3-oz veal cutlet (1/2" thick)	Two 3-oz veal cutlets (1/2" thick)
1/2 cup spaghetti sauce	1 cup spaghetti sauce
1 can (2 oz) mushroom stems and pieces, drained	1 can (4 oz) mushroom stems and pieces, drained
Snipped parsley	Snipped parsley

Pound veal cutlet[**s**] to ¼" thickness; cut into halves. Place veal in 22-oz casserole [**8 × 8 × 2" dish**]; top with spaghetti sauce. Cover with waxed paper and microwave on medium (275 watts) 2½ min [**4½ min**]; turn veal. Cover and microwave until veal is tender, 2½ to 5 min longer [**4½ to 6½ min longer**]. Top with mushrooms. Cover and microwave until hot, 30 to 60 sec [**1½ to 2 min**]. Sprinkle with parsley. Sprinkle with grated Parmesan cheese and serve on hot cooked linguine if desired.

Fish Fillet with Lemon Sauce

Fish Fillet with Lemon Sauce

1 Serving	[2 Servings]
1 fresh or frozen (thawed) fish fillet (3 oz)	2 fresh or frozen (thawed) fish fillets (3 oz each)
Dash of salt	1/8 tsp salt
Dash of white pepper	Dash of white pepper
1 tbsp margarine or butter, melted	2 tbsp margarine or butter, melted
1½ tsp lemon juice	1 tbsp lemon juice
1 tsp snipped parsley	2 tsp snipped parsley
Dash of paprika	1/8 tsp paprika

Pat fish fillet[s] dry. Place fish in 12-oz shallow casserole [**20-oz shallow casserole, with thickest parts to outside edge**]. Sprinkle with salt and pepper. Mix remaining ingredients; pour over fish. Cover with waxed paper and microwave on high (550 watts) until fish flakes easily with fork, 1 to 2 min [**2 to 3½ min**]. Fish should register 175° on meat thermometer. Sprinkle with additional snipped parsley. Serve with wild rice and lemon slices if desired.

Buttery Fish Fillet

1 Serving	[2 Servings]
1 fresh or frozen (thawed) fish fillet (3 oz)	2 fresh or frozen (thawed) fish fillets (3 oz each)
1 tbsp margarine or butter, melted	2 tbsp margarine or butter, melted
4 drops red pepper sauce	8 drops red pepper sauce
2 tbsp crushed round buttery crackers (4 crackers uncrushed)	1/4 cup crushed round buttery crackers (8 crackers uncrushed)
1/8 tsp salt	1/4 tsp salt
1/8 tsp paprika	1/4 tsp paprika

Pat fish fillet[s] dry. Mix margarine and pepper sauce. Mix cracker crumbs, salt and paprika. Dip fish into margarine mixture, then coat with cracker crumbs. Place on rack in 11 × 7 × 1½" dish [**with thickest parts to outside edges**]. Cover with waxed paper and microwave on high (550 watts) until fish flakes easily with fork, 1 to 2½ min [**2½ to 4 min**]. Fish should register 175° on meat thermometer. Garnish with lemon slices if desired.

Haddock Caribbean

1 Serving	[2 Servings]
1 piece (3 oz) fresh or frozen (thawed) haddock	2 pieces (3 oz each) fresh or frozen (thawed) haddock
Dash of salt	1/8 tsp salt
Dash of pepper	Dash of pepper
1/8" slice medium onion, separated into rings	Two 1/8" slices medium onion, separated into rings
1/2 small tomato, cut into 4 wedges	1 small tomato, cut into 8 wedges
1 tsp lime juice	2 tsp lime juice
1 tsp olive oil or vegetable oil	2 tsp olive oil or vegetable oil
2 pitted green olives, sliced	4 pitted green olives, sliced
2 slices avocado	4 slices avocado
1 lime wedge	2 lime wedges

Place haddock piece[s] in 12-oz shallow casserole [**24-oz shallow casserole, with thickest parts to outside edge**]. Sprinkle with salt and pepper. Place onion and tomato on haddock; sprinkle with lime juice and oil. Top with olives. Cover loosely and microwave on high until haddock flakes easily with fork, 2 to 3 min [**4 to 5 min**]. Haddock should register 175° on meat thermometer. Serve with avocado and lime.

Italian-style Flounder

1 Serving	[2 Servings]
1 piece (3 oz) fresh or frozen (thawed) flounder fillet	2 pieces (3 oz each) fresh or frozen (thawed) flounder fillet
Dash of salt	1/8 tsp salt
Dash of dried oregano leaves	1/4 tsp dried oregano leaves
Dash of paprika	Dash of paprika
1 tomato slice (1/2" thick)	2 tomato slices (1/2" thick)
1/2 tsp snipped chives	1 tsp snipped chives
1 tbsp Italian salad dressing	2 tbsp Italian salad dressing
1 tsp grated Parmesan cheese	2 tsp grated Parmesan cheese

Pat flounder piece[s] dry. Place flounder on rack in 11 × 7 × 1½" dish [**with thickest parts to outside edges**]. Sprinkle with salt, oregano and paprika. Place tomato slice[s] on flounder piece[s]; sprinkle with chives. Pour dressing over top; sprinkle with cheese. Cover loosely and microwave on high (550 watts) until flounder flakes easily with fork, 2 to 3 min [**4 to 5 min**]. Flounder should register 175° on meat thermometer.

Sole on Deviled Stuffing

1 Serving	[2 Servings]
1 piece (3 oz) fresh or frozen (thawed) sole fillet	2 pieces (3 oz each) fresh or frozen (thawed) sole fillet
1½ tsp margarine	1 tbsp margarine
1 tsp lemon juice	2 tsp lemon juice
1/8 tsp dry mustard	1/4 tsp dry mustard
1/8 tsp chili powder	1/4 tsp chili powder
1/8 tsp salt	1/4 tsp salt
1/8 tsp instant minced onion	1/4 tsp instant minced onion
1/4 cup soft bread crumbs	1/2 cup soft bread crumbs
1 tsp margarine or butter, melted	2 tsp margarine or butter, melted
1/8 tsp paprika	1/4 tsp paprika

Pat sole fillet[s] dry. Mix 1½ tsp [**1 tbsp**] margarine, the lemon juice, mustard, chili powder, salt and onion; stir in bread crumbs. Spread in 12-oz shallow casserole [**two 12-oz shallow casseroles**]. Place sole on top. Mix 1 tsp [**2 tsp**] margarine and the paprika; spread over sole. Cover with waxed paper and microwave on high (550 watts) until sole flakes easily with fork, 1 to 2 min [**2 to 3 min**]. Sole should register 175° on meat thermometer.

Halibut with Tomato Sauce

1 Serving	[2 Servings]
1 fresh or frozen (thawed) halibut steak (4 oz)	2 fresh or frozen (thawed) halibut steaks (4 oz each)
2 tbsp lemon juice	1/4 cup lemon juice
2 tbsp water	1/4 cup water
1/4 tsp garlic powder	1/2 tsp garlic powder
1 small tomato, chopped	1 large tomato, chopped
1 green onion (with top), chopped	2 green onions (with tops), chopped
1/8 tsp dried basil leaves	1/4 tsp dried basil leaves
1/8 tsp salt	1/4 tsp salt

Place halibut steak[s] in 10-oz shallow casserole [**20-oz shallow casserole**]. Mix lemon juice, water and garlic powder; pour over halibut. Cover and refrigerate, spooning liquid over halibut occasionally, at least 1 hour; drain.

Mix remaining ingredients; spoon over halibut. Cover with waxed paper and microwave on high (550 watts) until halibut flakes easily with fork, 3 to 5 min [**5 to 7 min**]. Halibut should register 175° on meat thermometer. Garnish with lemon wedges and parsley if desired.

Wine-poached Salmon Steak

1 Serving	[2 Servings]
Prepare Wine-poached Salmon Steak for 2 Servings. Serve any remaining salmon at another meal.	6-oz fresh or frozen (thawed) salmon steak
	2 tbsp dry white wine
	2 tbsp water
	1/8 tsp salt
	1/8 tsp pepper
	1/8 tsp dried thyme leaves
	1/8 tsp dried tarragon leaves
	2 lemon slices

Place salmon steak in 14-oz shallow casserole. Sprinkle with wine, water, salt, pepper, thyme and tarragon. Top with lemon slices. Cover with waxed paper and microwave on high (550 watts) until salmon flakes easily with fork, 3 to 5 min. Salmon should register 175° on meat thermometer. Remove from casserole before serving.

Crab Coquille

	1 Serving	[2 Servings]
	1½ tsp margarine or butter	1 tbsp margarine or butter
	1 green onion (with top), thinly sliced	2 green onions (with tops), thinly sliced
	½ tsp cornstarch	1 tsp cornstarch
	¼ cup half-and-half	½ cup half-and-half
	1 tsp lemon juice	2 tsp lemon juice
	Dash of salt	⅛ tsp salt
	Dash of white pepper	⅛ tsp white pepper
	⅓ cup cooked crabmeat	⅔ cup cooked crabmeat
	2 mushrooms, thinly sliced	4 mushrooms, thinly sliced
	1 tbsp dry bread crumbs	2 tbsp dry bread crumbs
	2 tsp grated Parmesan cheese	1 tbsp plus 1 tsp grated Parmesan cheese
	1½ tsp margarine or butter, melted	1 tbsp margarine or butter, melted

Place 1½ tsp [**1 tbsp**] margarine and the onion[**s**] in 2-cup measure [**4-cup measure**]. Microwave uncovered on high (550 watts) until crisp-tender, 1 to 2 min [**2 to 3 min**]. Mix in cornstarch. Stir in half-and-half, lemon juice, salt and pepper. Microwave uncovered 30 sec [**1 min**]; stir. Microwave uncovered until thickened, about 30 sec longer [**about 1 min longer**]. Stir in crabmeat and mushrooms. Spoon into baking shell [**2 baking shells**] or 12-oz shallow casserole [**two 12-oz shallow casseroles**]. Mix bread crumbs, cheese and 1½ tsp [**1 tbsp**] margarine. Sprinkle over top[**s**]. Cover loosely and microwave until hot 1 to 2 min [**2 to 3 min**].

Crab Coquilles

Salmon Tetrazzini

1 Serving	[2 Servings]
1 tsp dry white wine	2 tsp dry white wine
Milk	Milk
½ can (7¾-oz size) salmon, drained (reserve 2 tbsp liquid)	1 can (7¾ oz) salmon, drained (reserve ¼ cup liquid)
1½ tsp margarine or butter	1 tbsp margarine or butter
1½ tsp all-purpose flour	1 tbsp all-purpose flour
⅛ tsp salt	¼ tsp salt
¾ cup hot cooked spaghetti	1½ cups hot cooked spaghetti
1 tbsp grated Parmesan cheese	2 tbsp grated Parmesan cheese
Dash of ground nutmeg	⅛ tsp ground nutmeg
2 mushrooms, sliced	4 mushrooms, sliced
1 tbsp toasted sliced almonds (page 8)	2 tbsp toasted sliced almonds (page 8)

Add wine and enough milk to reserved salmon liquid to measure ½ cup [1 cup]; reserve. Microwave margarine uncovered in 24-oz casserole [1-qt casserole] on high (550 watts) until melted, about 30 sec [about 45 sec]. Mix in flour. Stir in salt and reserved wine mixture. Microwave uncovered, stirring every 30 sec, until thickened, 2½ to 3 min [3 to 4 min]. Stir in salmon, spaghetti, cheese, nutmeg and mushrooms. Sprinkle with almonds. Microwave uncovered until hot, 2 to 2½ min [5 to 6 min].

Oysters with Spinach Noodles

1 Serving	[2 Servings]
1 carton (8 oz) shucked fresh oysters, drained (½ cup)	2 cartons (8 oz each) shucked fresh oysters, drained (1 cup)
¾ cup hot cooked spinach noodles	1½ cups hot cooked spinach noodles
3 tbsp dairy sour cream	⅓ cup dairy sour cream
2 tbsp milk	¼ cup milk
⅛ tsp salt	¼ tsp salt
Dash of white pepper	⅛ tsp white pepper
1 green onion (with top), chopped	2 green onions (with tops), chopped
1½ tsp margarine or butter, melted	1 tbsp margarine or butter, melted
1½ tsp grated Romano or Parmesan cheese	1 tbsp grated Romano or Parmesan cheese

Place oysters in 15-oz casserole [22-oz casserole]. Cover with waxed paper and microwave on high (550 watts) until edges of oysters begin to curl, 1 to 2 min [3 to 4 min, stirring after 2 min]; drain. Mix in noodles, sour cream, milk, salt, pepper and onion[s].

Sprinkle with margarine and cheese. Cover with waxed paper and microwave until hot, 2 to 3 min [2 to 4 min].

Salmon Tetrazzini

Gingered Scallops

1 Serving	[2 Servings]
1 tbsp chopped green onion (with top)	2 tbsp chopped green onion (with top)
1½ tsp margarine or butter	1 tbsp margarine or butter
1½ tsp all-purpose flour	1 tbsp all-purpose flour
¼ cup half-and-half	½ cup half-and-half
1 tbsp dry white wine	2 tbsp dry white wine
¼ tsp grated gingerroot	½ tsp grated gingerroot
⅛ tsp salt	¼ tsp salt
3 oz bay scallops or sea scallops, cut into ½" pieces (⅓ cup)	6 oz bay scallops or sea scallops, cut into ½" pieces (⅔ cup)
1 jar (2½ oz) whole mushrooms, drained	1 jar (4½ oz) whole mushrooms, drained

Place onion and margarine in 2-cup measure [**4-cup measure**]. Microwave uncovered on high (550 watts) until margarine is melted, about 30 sec [**about 1 min**]. Mix in flour, Stir in half-and-half, wine, gingerroot and salt. Microwave uncovered 30 sec [**1 min**]; stir. Microwave until thickened, about 30 sec longer [**about 1 min longer**]. Stir in scallops and mushrooms. Spoon into 14-oz shallow casserole [**two 14-oz shallow casseroles**]. Cover tightly and microwave on medium-high (385 watts), rotating casserole[**s**] ½ turn every min, until bubbly, 2 to 3 min [**4 to 5 min**]. Garnish with pimiento and serve with hot cooked rice if desired.

Shrimp-Egg Scramble

1 Serving	[2 Servings]
¼ cup milk	½ cup milk
1 egg	2 eggs
1 tbsp dry white wine	2 tbsp dry white wine
1 tsp snipped parsley	2 tsp snipped parsley
⅛ tsp dry mustard	¼ tsp dry mustard
Dash of salt	⅛ tsp salt
Dash of pepper	⅛ tsp pepper
¾ cup soft bread cubes (1 slice bread)	1½ cups soft bread cubes (2 slices bread)
¼ cup shredded process sharp American cheese	½ cup shredded process sharp American cheese
¼ cup chopped cooked shrimp	½ cup chopped cooked shrimp

Beat milk and egg[**s**] with fork in 2-cup measure [**4-cup measure**]. Beat in wine, parsley, mustard, salt and pepper. Microwave uncovered on medium-high (385 watts) 30 sec; stir. Microwave uncovered until hot, 30 to 60 sec longer [**30 sec to 1½ min longer**]. Stir in remaining ingredients. Pour into 10-oz casserole [**two 10-oz casseroles**]. Cover with waxed paper and microwave on inverted saucer[**s**] on medium (275 watts) 1 min [**2 min**]; stir. Cover with waxed paper and microwave until center is set, 2½ to 4 min [**6 to 8 min**]. Serve with lemon wedges if desired.

Gingered Scallops

Tuna-Mushroom Casserole

1 Serving	[2 Servings]
½ cup hot cooked noodles	1 cup hot cooked noodles
½ can (6½-oz size) tuna, drained	1 can (6½-oz) tuna, drained
3 tbsp dairy sour cream	⅓ cup dairy sour cream
2 tbsp milk	¼ cup milk
⅛ tsp salt	¼ tsp salt
Dash of pepper	⅛ tsp pepper
½ jar (2½-oz size) sliced mushrooms, drained	1 jar (2½ oz) sliced mushrooms, drained
1 tbsp dry bread crumbs	2 tbsp dry bread crumbs
1 tbsp grated Parmesan cheese	2 tbsp grated Parmesan cheese
1½ tsp margarine or butter, melted	1 tbsp margarine or butter, melted
Snipped parsley	Snipped parsley

Mix noodles, tuna, sour cream, milk, salt, pepper and mushrooms in 15-oz casserole [**1-qt casserole**]. Cover tightly and microwave on medium (275 watts) 2 min [**3 min**]; stir.

Mix bread crumbs, cheese and margarine; sprinkle over tuna mixture. Microwave uncovered until hot, 2½ to 4 min [**5 to 6 min**]. Sprinkle with parsley.

Spaghetti with Tuna Sauce

1 Serving	[2 Servings]
1½ tsp margarine or butter	1 tbsp margarine or butter
½ small clove garlic, finely chopped	1 small clove garlic, finely chopped
¼ cup half-and-half	½ cup half-and-half
1 tbsp grated Parmesan cheese	2 tbsp grated Parmesan cheese
⅛ tsp dried oregano leaves	¼ tsp dried oregano leaves
⅛ tsp salt	¼ tsp salt
⅛ tsp white pepper	¼ tsp white pepper
½ can (6½-oz size) tuna, drained	1 can (6½ oz) tuna, drained
4 ripe olives, sliced	8 ripe olives, sliced
¾ cup hot cooked thin spaghetti	1½ cups hot cooked thin spaghetti

Place margarine and garlic in 2-cup measure [**4-cup measure**]. Microwave uncovered on high (550 watts) until margarine is melted, about 30 sec [**about 45 sec**]. Stir in remaining ingredients except spaghetti. Cover with waxed paper and microwave until bubbly, 1½ to 2 min [**2½ to 3 min**]. Toss with hot spaghetti. Sprinkle with snipped parsley and Parmesan cheese if desired.

Chicken and Artichoke Casserole

Chicken and Artichoke Casserole

1 Serving	[2 Servings]
1/3 cup coarsely cut-up cooked chicken	2/3 cup coarsely cut-up cooked chicken
1/3 cup instant rice	2/3 cup instant rice
1/3 cup hot water	2/3 cup hot water
1/2 tsp instant chicken bouillon	1 tsp instant chicken bouillon
2 tbsp sliced pimiento-stuffed olives	1/4 cup sliced pimiento-stuffed olives
2 tbsp shredded Swiss cheese	1/4 cup shredded Swiss cheese
Dash of pepper	Dash of pepper
1/2 jar (6-oz size) marinated artichoke hearts, drained and cut into halves	1 jar (6 oz) marinated artichoke hearts, drained and cut into halves

Mix all ingredients in 16-oz casserole [**1-qt casserole**]. Cover tightly and microwave on high (550 watts) 2 min [**3 min**]; stir. Cover tightly and microwave until liquid is absorbed, 2 to 3 min longer [**2 to 3 min longer**]. Sprinkle with paprika if desired.

Chicken and Spinach Noodles

1 Serving	[2 Servings]
3/4 cup hot cooked spinach noodles	1 1/2 cups hot cooked spinach noodles
1/3 cup coarsely cut-up cooked chicken	2/3 cup coarsely cut-up cooked chicken
2 tbsp grated Romano cheese	1/4 cup grated Romano cheese
1 tbsp milk	2 tbsp milk
1 tbsp finely chopped onion	2 tbsp finely chopped onion
1 tbsp margarine or butter	2 tbsp margarine or butter
1/8 tsp salt	1/4 tsp salt
Dash of pepper	1/8 tsp pepper
1 can (2 oz) mushroom stems and pieces, drained	1 can (4 oz) mushroom stems and pieces, drained

Mix all ingredients in 16-oz casserole [**1-qt casserole**]. Cover tightly and microwave on high (550 watts) 1 min [**2 min**]; stir. Cover tightly and microwave until chicken is hot, 1 1/2 to 2 1/2 min longer [**2 to 3 min longer**]. Serve with grated Romano cheese and garnish with parsley if desired.

Oriental-style Chicken Rice

	1 Serving	[2 Servings]

1 Serving

1 can (2 oz) mushroom stems and pieces, drained (reserve liquid)
⅓ cup coarsely cut-up cooked chicken
⅓ cup uncooked instant rice
2 tbsp chopped water chestnuts
2 tbsp chopped green onions (with tops)
2 tsp soy sauce
1½ tsp margarine or butter
Dash of pepper

[2 Servings]

1 can (4 oz) mushroom stems and pieces, drained (reserve liquid)
⅔ cup coarsely cut-up cooked chicken
⅔ cup uncooked instant rice
¼ cup chopped water chestnuts
¼ cup chopped green onions (with tops)
1 tbsp plus 1 tsp soy sauce
1 tbsp margarine or butter
⅛ tsp pepper

Add enough hot water to reserved mushroom liquid to measure ⅓ cup [⅔ cup]. Pour into 15-oz casserole [1-qt casserole]; stir in remaining ingredients. Cover tightly and microwave on high (550 watts) 1 min [2 min]; stir. Cover and microwave until rice is tender and liquid is absorbed, 2 to 3 min [2 to 4 min].

Poached Chicken Breast

Place 8-oz chicken breast half, skin side up, in 1-qt casserole. Cover tightly and microwave on high (550 watts) until done, 3½ to 4 min. Refrigerate until cool enough to handle, about 10 min.

Slice and serve, or skin chicken, remove meat from bones and cut up or use in recipes that call for cooked chicken.

Microwaving Chicken Pieces

Brush chicken piece[s] with equal parts browning sauce and water. Or, if desired, dip chicken piece[s] into melted margarine or butter, then coat with crushed seasoned crumbs. Place chicken piece[s], skin side[s] up, on rack in 11 × 7 × 1½" dish [with thickest parts to outside edges]. Cover with waxed paper and microwave until done as directed below. For 2 Servings, rearrange chicken pieces halfway through microwave time, keeping thickest parts toward outside edges of dish.

Chicken Part	1 Serving	[2 Servings]	Microwave Procedure
Breast with ribs	1 half (6 oz)	2 halves (6 oz each)	Microwave on high (550 watts) 3½ to 4½ min [5½ to 6½ min].
Drumstick	1 (3 oz)	2 (3 oz each)	Microwave on medium-high (385 watts) 5 to 6 min [8 to 9 min].
Thigh	1 (3 oz)	2 (3 oz each)	Microwave on medium-high (385 watts) 5 to 6 min [8 to 10 min].

Chicken a la King

1 Serving	[2 Servings]
1 tbsp margarine or butter	2 tbsp margarine or butter
1/2 tsp instant chicken bouillon	1 tsp instant chicken bouillon
1 tbsp all-purpose flour	2 tbsp all-purpose flour
1/8 tsp salt	1/4 tsp salt
Dash of white pepper	Dash of white pepper
1/2 cup milk	1 cup milk
1 tsp dry white wine	2 tsp dry white wine
1/3 cup coarsely cut-up cooked chicken	2/3 cup coarsely cut-up cooked chicken
1 tsp chopped pimientos	2 tsp chopped pimientos
1/2 tsp parsley flakes	1 tsp parsley flakes
1 can (2 oz) mushroom stems and pieces, drained	1 can (4 oz) mushroom stems and pieces, drained

Place margarine and bouillon (dry) in 2-cup measure [**4-cup measure**]. Microwave uncovered on high (550 watts) until margarine is melted, about 30 sec [**about 45 sec**]. Mix in flour, salt and pepper. Stir in milk and wine. Microwave uncovered on medium-high (385 watts) 1 min [**2 min**]; stir. Microwave uncovered until thickened, 1 to 2 min longer [**3½ to 4½ min longer**]. Stir in remaining ingredients. Cover tightly and microwave on high (550 watts) until hot, 1½ to 2 min [**2 to 3 min**]. Serve over baking powder biscuit[**s**] if desired.

Chicken-filled Tomato

1 Serving	[2 Servings]
1 firm medium tomato	2 firm medium tomatoes
1/4 cup finely cut-up cooked chicken	1/2 cup finely cut-up cooked chicken
1 tbsp finely chopped onion	2 tbsp finely chopped onion
1 tbsp finely chopped green pepper	2 tbsp finely chopped green pepper
1½ tsp margarine or butter	1 tbsp margarine or butter
1/8 tsp salt	1/4 tsp salt
Dash of pepper	1/8 tsp pepper
1 tsp lemon juice	2 tsp lemon juice

Remove stem end[**s**] from tomato[**es**]. Remove pulp, leaving 3/8" wall[**s**]. Chop tomato pulp; place in 10-oz casserole [**22-oz casserole**]. Mix in chicken, onion, green pepper, margarine, salt and pepper. Cover loosely and microwave on high (550 watts) until hot, 1 to 1¼ min [**1½ to 2½ min**].

Fill tomato[**es**] with chicken mixture; place in same casserole. Sprinkle with lemon juice. Cover loosely and microwave on high (550 watts) until chicken mixture and tomato[**es**] are warm, 1 to 1¼ min [**2 to 3½ min**]. Garnish with watercress if desired.

Chicken-filled Tomatoes

Chicken Kabobs

1 Serving	[2 Servings]
½ chicken breast half (3 oz), boned and skinned	1 chicken breast half (6 oz), boned and skinned
1 tbsp soy sauce	2 tbsp soy sauce
1 tbsp water	2 tbsp water
1 tbsp vegetable oil	2 tbsp vegetable oil
⅛ tsp ground ginger	¼ tsp ground ginger
⅓ green pepper, cut into 1" pieces	⅔ green pepper, cut into 1" pieces
2 dried figs, cut into halves	4 dried figs, cut into halves
1 cherry tomato, cut into halves	2 cherry tomatoes, cut into halves

Cut chicken into 1" pieces. Mix chicken, soy sauce, water, oil and ginger in bowl. Cover and refrigerate 15 min. Drain chicken, reserving marinade.

Alternate green pepper pieces with chicken and fig halves on two 10" wooden skewers [**four 10" wooden skewers**]. Place kabobs in $10 \times 6 \times 1\frac{1}{2}$" dish; brush with reserved marinade. Cover with waxed paper and microwave on high (550 watts) 1 min [**2 min**]; rearrange kabobs. Cover with waxed paper and microwave until chicken is done, 30 to 60 seconds longer [**1 to 2 min longer**]. Place cherry tomato half on end of each skewer. Microwave uncovered until warm, 20 to 30 sec [**45 to 60 sec**]. Serve with lemon wedges if desired.

Chicken Kiev

1 Serving	[2 Servings]
1 tbsp margarine or butter, softened	2 tbsp margarine or butter, softened
½ tsp snipped chives	1 tsp snipped chives
Dash of garlic powder	⅛ tsp garlic powder
Dash of white pepper	⅛ tsp white pepper
½ chicken breast half (3 oz), boned and skinned	1 chicken breast half (6 oz), boned, skinned and cut into halves
½ cup corn flake cereal, crushed (3 tbsp)	1 cup corn flake cereal, crushed (⅓ cup)
¼ tsp dried tarragon leaves, crushed	½ tsp dried tarragon leaves, crushed
⅛ tsp paprika	¼ tsp paprika
1 tbsp buttermilk or milk	2 tbsp buttermilk or milk

Mix margarine, chives, garlic powder and pepper; shape into 1" square [**two 1" squares**]. Wrap and freeze until firm, about 20 min.

Pound chicken piece[**s**] to ¼" thickness between pieces of waxed paper. Place square[**s**] of margarine mixture on center of chicken piece[**s**]. Fold long sides over margarine; fold ends up and secure with wooden picks. Mix cereal, tarragon and paprika. Dip chicken into buttermilk; coat evenly with cereal mixture. Place chicken, seam side[**s**] up, on rack in $11 \times 7 \times 1\frac{1}{2}$" dish. Cover with waxed paper and microwave on high (550 watts) until done, 3 to 4 min [**5 to 6 min**]. Remove wooden picks. Spoon melted margarine mixture over top[**s**].

Italian-style Chicken

1 Serving	[2 Servings]
1/2 chicken breast half (3 oz), skinned	**1 chicken breast half (6 oz), skinned**
1/2 can (7 1/2-oz size) whole tomatoes, undrained	**1 can (7 1/2 oz) whole tomatoes, undrained**
1 tsp all-purpose flour	**2 tsp all-purpose flour**
1 tbsp chopped onion	**2 tbsp chopped onion**
1/4 tsp salt	**1/2 tsp salt**
1/4 tsp dried oregano leaves	**1/2 tsp dried oregano leaves**
Dash of pepper	**1/8 tsp pepper**
1/2 small clove garlic, finely chopped	**1 small clove garlic, finely chopped**
1/4 cup sliced mushrooms	**1/2 cup sliced mushrooms**
1 tbsp sliced pitted ripe olives	**2 tbsp sliced pitted ripe olives**
3/4 cup hot cooked spaghetti	**1 1/2 cups hot cooked spaghetti**

Place chicken breast piece[s], meaty side[s] down, in 22-oz casserole [**1-qt casserole**]. Mix tomatoes and flour; break up tomatoes. Stir in onion, salt, oregano, pepper and garlic; pour over chicken. Cover with waxed paper and microwave on high (550 watts) until thickest part of chicken is done, 3 1/2 to 4 1/2 min [**5 to 6 min**]. Add mushrooms and olives. Spoon sauce over top. Cover and microwave until mushrooms are hot, 30 to 60 sec [**1 to 2 min**]. Serve on spaghetti.

Fruited Chicken

1 Serving	[2 Servings]
1/2 chicken breast half (3 oz), skinned	**1 chicken breast half (6 oz), skinned and cut into halves**
1 tsp margarine or butter, softened	**2 tsp margarine or butter, softened**
1/4 tsp paprika	**1/2 tsp paprika**
1/2 can (8-oz size) pineapple chunks in juice, undrained	**1 can (8 oz) pineapple chunks in juice, undrained**
1/2 small orange, pared and sectioned	**1 small orange, pared and sectioned**
1 1/2 tsp raisins	**1 tbsp raisins**
1 tsp cornstarch	**2 tsp cornstarch**
1/8 tsp salt	**1/4 tsp salt**
Dash of ground cinnamon	**1/8 tsp ground cinnamon**
Dash of ground cloves	**Dash of ground cloves**

Rub chicken piece[s] with margarine and paprika. Place in 14-oz shallow casserole [**two 14-oz shallow casseroles**]. Cover with waxed paper and microwave on high (550 watts) until thickest parts are done, 1 to 2 min [**2 to 3 min**]. Mix remaining ingredients; spoon over chicken. Cover with waxed paper and microwave until fruit is hot, 1 1/2 to 2 min [**1 1/2 to 3 min**]. Garnish with parsley if desired.

Curried Chicken and Tomatoes

1 Serving	[2 Servings]
½ chicken breast half (3 oz), boned and skinned	1 chicken breast half (6 oz), boned, skinned and cut into halves
1 tbsp margarine or butter	2 tbsp margarine or butter
1 tbsp chopped onion	2 tbsp chopped onion
½ tsp curry powder	1 tsp curry powder
½ tsp lemon juice	1 tsp lemon juice
⅛ tsp salt	¼ tsp salt
½ small clove garlic, finely chopped	1 small clove garlic, finely chopped
4 drops red pepper sauce	¼ tsp red pepper sauce
½ can (7½-oz size) whole tomatoes, drained	1 can (7½ oz) whole tomatoes, drained
¾ cup hot cooked rice	1½ cups hot cooked rice

Cut chicken into ¼" strips. Mix chicken and remaining ingredients except rice in 15-oz casserole [**1-qt casserole**]; break up tomatoes. Cover loosely and microwave on high (550 watts) 1 min [**2 min**]; stir. Cover loosely and microwave until chicken is done, 1 to 2 min [**2 to 4 min**]. Serve over rice. Garnish with chopped peanuts, green onion and chutney if desired.

Mexican-style Chicken

1 Serving	[2 Servings]
1 chicken thigh (3 oz)	2 chicken thighs (3 oz each)
3 tbsp tomato sauce	⅓ cup tomato sauce
¼ tsp parsley flakes	½ tsp parsley flakes
¼ tsp chili powder	½ tsp chili powder
⅛ tsp sugar	¼ tsp sugar
Dash of salt	⅛ tsp salt
4 drops red pepper sauce	⅛ tsp red pepper sauce

Place chicken thigh[**s**], skin side[**s**] up, in 14-oz shallow casserole [**22-oz shallow casserole, with thickest parts to outside edge**]. Mix remaining ingredients; spread over chicken. Cover with waxed paper and microwave on medium-high (385 watts) until thickest parts of chicken are done, 4 to 6 min [**9 to 11 min**]. Serve with buttered warm flour tortillas if desired.

Chicken Wings with Peppers

1 Serving	[2 Servings]
2 chicken wings (3 oz each), tips removed	**4 chicken wings (3 oz each), tips removed**
2 tbsp dry red wine	**1/4 cup dry red wine**
1 tsp packed brown sugar	**2 tsp packed brown sugar**
1 1/2 tsp soy sauce	**1 tbsp soy sauce**
1/4 tsp instant chicken bouillon	**1/2 tsp instant chicken bouillon**
1/4 green pepper, cut into 1/4" strips	**1/2 green pepper, cut into 1/4" strips**
1/4 red pepper, cut into 1/4" strips	**1/2 red pepper, cut into 1/4" strips**
1 green onion (with top), cut into 2" pieces	**2 green onions (with tops), cut into 2" pieces**

Place chicken wings in 22-oz casserole [**8 × 8 × 2" dish**]. Mix wine, brown sugar, soy sauce and bouillon (dry); pour over chicken. Cover with waxed paper and microwave on medium-high (385 watts) until almost done, 2 to 3 min [**5 to 7 min**]. Rotate dish 1/2 turn; add remaining ingredients. Cover with waxed paper and microwave until chicken is done and vegetables are crisp-tender, 3 to 5 min [**8 to 10 min**]. Serve with hot cooked rice if desired.

Wine-Barbecue Chicken Drumstick

1 Serving	[2 Servings]
1 chicken drumstick (3 oz)	**2 chicken drumsticks (3 oz each)**
1 tbsp barbecue sauce	**3 tbsp barbecue sauce**
1 tsp dry red wine	**1 tbsp dry red wine**
Dash of garlic salt	**Dash of garlic salt**
Dash of pepper	**Dash of pepper**

Place chicken drumstick[**s**] in 16-oz shallow casserole. Mix remaining ingredients; pour over chicken. Cover with waxed paper and microwave on medium-high (385 watts) until done, 3 to 4 min [**6 to 8 min**]. Spoon sauce over chicken.

Cornish Hen Bourguignon

1 Serving	[2 Servings]
Prepare Cornish Hen Bourguignon for 2 Servings. Reheat half of the hen for another meal. See Main Dish Reheat Chart, page 83.	¼ tsp salt
	¼ tsp paprika
	⅛ tsp pepper
	Dash of ground nutmeg
	1¼- lb Rock Cornish hen, thawed
	¼ cup dry red wine
	1 tsp snipped parsley
	½ tsp instant chicken bouillon
	¼ tsp instant minced onion
	1 slice bacon, cut into halves
	1 cup hot cooked brown or white rice
	2 tsp currant jelly

Mix salt, paprika, pepper and nutmeg; rub over outside and cavity of Rock Cornish hen. Fold neck skin under back of hen. Tie drumsticks together. Place hen, breast side down, on rack in 11 × 7 × 1½" dish. Mix wine, parsley, bouillon (dry) and onion; pour half of the mixture over hen. Cover with waxed paper and microwave on high (550 watts) 5 min. Turn hen over; crisscross bacon halves on top. Pour remaining wine mixture over hen. Cover with waxed paper and microwave until done, 6 to 8 min.

Remove hen to warm platter. Remove bacon and cut into small pieces; stir into rice. Remove rack from dish. Stir jelly into mixture in dish. Microwave uncovered, stirring twice, until jelly is melted, 2 to 3 min. Skim off fat. To serve, cut hen into halves with kitchen scissors, cutting through breast and along backbone from tail to neck. Place on rice; pour sauce over top. Garnish with Tomato Rose (below) if desired.

Tomato Rose

Pare small tomato. Cut thin spiral of tomato; curl to resemble rose.

Turkey Enchiladas

1 Serving	[2 Servings]
⅓ cup cut-up cooked turkey	⅔ cup cut-up cooked turkey
⅓ cup chopped tomato	⅔ cup chopped tomato
2 tbsp sliced green onion	¼ cup sliced green onions
1 tsp chopped green chilies, drained	2 tsp chopped green chilies, drained
Dash of garlic powder	⅛ tsp garlic powder
Two 6" flour tortillas	Four 6" flour tortillas
2 tbsp green taco sauce	¼ cup green taco sauce
2 tbsp shredded Monterey Jack cheese	¼ cup shredded Monterey Jack cheese
1 tbsp chopped ripe olives	2 tbsp chopped ripe olives

Mix turkey, tomato, onions, chilies and garlic powder in 15-oz casserole. Cover tightly and microwave on high (550 watts) 1 min; stir. Cover tightly and microwave until hot, 30 to 60 seconds longer [1 to 2 min longer]; drain.

Place tortillas in 1 stack [2 stacks] on plate[s]. Cover with waxed paper and microwave on medium (275 watts) until softened, 15 to 20 sec [25 to 30 sec]. Spread about ⅓ cup turkey mixture on each tortilla; top with 1 tbsp taco sauce. Roll tortillas around turkey mixture. Arrange tortillas, seam sides down, in 15-oz shallow casserole [two 15-oz shallow casseroles]. Sprinkle with cheese and olives. Cover with waxed paper and microwave on high (550 watts) until enchiladas are hot and cheese is melted, 1 to 2 min [2 to 3 min]. Serve with additional taco sauce and dairy sour cream if desired.

Cornish Hen Bourguignon

Turkey Casserole

1 Serving	[2 Servings]
½ can (7½-oz size) semicondensed cream of mushroom soup	1 can (7½ oz) semicondensed cream of mushroom soup
2 tbsp milk	¼ cup milk
1½ tsp instant minced onion	1 tbsp instant minced onion
Dash of pepper	⅛ tsp pepper
½ cup coarsely cut-up cooked turkey	1 cup coarsely cut-up cooked turkey
¼ cup crushed corn chips	½ cup crushed corn chips
1 tbsp shredded Cheddar cheese	2 tbsp shredded Cheddar cheese

Mix soup, milk, onion and pepper in 2-cup measure [4-cup measure]. Cover tightly and microwave on high (550 watts) 1 min; stir. Cover tightly and microwave until hot and bubbly, 30 to 60 sec longer [1½ to 2½ min longer]. Stir in turkey.

Place corn chips in 12-oz casserole [22-oz casserole]; spoon turkey mixture over top.

Microwave uncovered on high (550 watts) until hot and bubbly, 1½ to 3 min [3 to 5 min]. Sprinkle with cheese. Serve with cranberry relish if desired.

Turkey Divan

1 Serving	[2 Servings]
1 tbsp margarine or butter	2 tbsp margarine or butter
½ tsp instant chicken bouillon	1 tsp instant chicken bouillon
1 tbsp all-purpose flour	2 tbsp all-purpose flour
⅓ cup half-and-half	⅔ cup half-and-half
1 tbsp dry white wine	2 tbsp dry white wine
½ can (10½-oz size) cut asparagus spears, drained	1 can (10½ oz) cut asparagus spears, drained
2 slices (1½ oz each) cooked turkey	4 slices (1½ oz each) cooked turkey
1 tsp grated Parmesan cheese	2 tsp grated Parmesan cheese

Place margarine and bouillon (dry) in 2-cup measure [4-cup measure]. Microwave uncovered on high (550 watts) until margarine is melted, about 30 sec [about 45 sec]. Mix in flour. Stir in half-and-half and wine. Microwave uncovered on medium-high (385 watts) 30 sec; stir. Microwave uncovered until sauce is thickened, 1 to 1½ min longer [2 to 3½ min longer].

Place asparagus in 15-oz shallow casserole [two 15-oz shallow casseroles]; arrange turkey on top. Pour sauce over turkey; sprinkle with cheese. Cover with waxed paper and microwave on medium-high (385 watts) until hot, 2 to 3 min [3 to 4 min].

Meal On A Plate

If you are in the mood for a cook and serve meal, these four dinners are just right for one or two. All the food is cooked on one plate and then served right from the microwave on the same dish. Just add a crisp green salad and a piece of fresh fruit for dessert — your meal is complete with very little clean-up.

Polish Sausage Dinner

1 Serving	[2 Servings]
1 medium Bermuda onion, peeled	*2 medium Bermuda onions, peeled*
1 tsp margarine or butter	*2 tsp margarine or butter*
1 tsp snipped parsley	*2 tsp snipped parsley*
⅛ tsp garlic salt	*¼ tsp garlic salt*
1 fully cooked Polish sausage	*2 fully cooked Polish sausages*
1 tbsp shredded mozzarella cheese	*2 tbsp shredded mozzarella cheese*
½ tomato, sliced	*1 tomato, sliced*
2 tsp Italian salad dressing	*1 tbsp plus 1 tsp Italian salad dressing*
Freshly ground pepper	*Freshly ground pepper*

Cut onion[s] into fourths to within ½ inch of bottom[s]. Place on 7½" plate [**two 7½" plates**]. Spread onion[s] apart slightly; top with margarine and sprinkle with parsley and garlic salt. Cover tightly and microwave on high (550 watts) until almost tender, 2 to 3 min [**4 to 5 min**]; rotate plate[s] ¼ turn. Microwave until tender, 1 to 2 min longer [**1½ to 2½ min longer**].

Cut sausage[s] lengthwise into halves. Place on plate[s] next to onion[s]. Cover tightly and microwave until sausage is hot 1 to 2 min [**1½ to 2½ min**]. Sprinkle cheese over sausage[s]. Place tomato on plate[s]; sprinkle with dressing and pepper. Microwave uncovered until cheese is melted, 1 to 1½ min [**1½ to 2 min**].

Chutney Ham Dinner

1 Serving	[2 Servings]
1 cup finely shredded cabbage	*2 cups finely shredded cabbage*
2 tbsp chopped green onion (with top)	*¼ cup chopped green onion (with tops)*
2 tbsp mayonnaise or salad dressing	*¼ cup mayonnaise or salad dressing*
1 tsp prepared mustard	*2 tsp prepared mustard*
⅛ tsp salt	*¼ tsp salt*
1 piece fully cooked smoked ham slice (3 oz), ¼" thick	*2 pieces fully cooked smoked ham slice (6 oz), ¼" thick*
2 tbsp chutney	*¼ cup chutney*
1 bran muffin	*2 bran muffins*

Mix cabbage, onion[s], mayonnaise, mustard and salt. Place on 7½" plate [**two 7½" plates**]. Place ham piece[s] next to cabbage. Cover tightly and microwave on high (550 watts) until ham is hot and cabbage is crisp-tender, 1½ to 2½ min [**3 to 4 min**]. Spread chutney over ham; place muffin[s] on plate[s]. Microwave uncovered until muffin is warm, 30 to 60 sec [**1 to 1½ min**].

Steak au Poivre Dinner

1 Serving	[2 Servings]
1 medium baking potato	2 medium baking
Salt	potatoes
1/8 tsp browning sauce	Salt
1 slice (3 oz) beef	1/4 tsp browning sauce
tenderloin (3/4" thick)	2 slices (3 oz each)
1/8 tsp peppercorns,	beef tenderloin
crushed	(3/4" thick)
1/2 can (8-oz size)	1/4 tsp peppercorns,
French-style green	crushed
beans, drained	1 can (8 oz)
1/4 tsp sesame seed	French-style green
Dash of garlic powder	beans, drained
1 tsp margarine or	1/2 tsp sesame seed
butter	1/8 tsp garlic powder
	2 tsp margarine or
	butter

Dampen potato[es]; sprinkle with salt. Prick with fork to allow steam to escape. Place potato[es] on 7½" plate [two 7½" plates]. Microwave uncovered on high (550 watts) until almost tender, 3 to 3½ min [6 to 7 min].

Brush browning sauce over both sides of beef tenderloin; press peppercorns into both sides. Place on plate[s] next to potato[es]; turn potato[es] over. Place beans on plate[s]; sprinkle with sesame seed and garlic powder. Dot with margarine. Cover with waxed paper and microwave on medium (275 watts) until meat thermometer inserted horizontally in beef registers 135°, 3½ to 4½ min [7 to 9½ min]. Top potato[es] with seasoned sour cream and snipped chives if desired.

Lemon Chicken Dinner

1 Serving	[2 Servings]
1/2 chicken breast half	1 chicken breast half
(3 oz), boned and	(6 oz), boned,
skinned	skinned and cut
1 tsp margarine or	into halves
butter, softened	2 tsp margarine or
1/8 tsp paprika	butter, softened
1/8 tsp grated lemon peel	1/4 tsp paprika
1/2 small green pepper,	1/4 tsp grated lemon
cut into 1/8" slices	peel
1/8" slice medium	1 small green pepper,
onion, separated into	cut into 1/8" slices
rings	Two 1/8" slices
1/8 tsp salt	medium onion,
Freshly ground pepper	separated into
1/2 medium tomato, cut	rings
into wedges	1/4 tsp salt
1 tbsp cream cheese,	Freshly ground
softened	pepper
Dash of dried dill	1 medium tomato, cut
weed	into wedges
1 Parker House roll	2 tbsp cream cheese,
	softened
	1/8 tsp dried dill weed
	2 Parker House rolls

Rub chicken breast piece[s] with margarine, paprika and lemon peel. Place on 7½" plate [two 7½" plates]. Cover with waxed paper and microwave on high (550 watts) until thickest part is almost done, 1½ to 3 min [3 to 4½ min]. Mix green pepper, onion and salt; place on plate[s] next to chicken. Sprinkle with pepper. Cover with waxed paper and microwave until vegetables are crisp-tender, 1½ to 2 min [2 to 2½ min]; add tomato to green pepper mixture. Cover and microwave until tomato is hot, 30 to 45 sec [45 to 60 sec].

Mix cream cheese and dill weed; spread in break[s] of roll[s]. Place roll[s] on plate[s]. Microwave uncovered until warm, 15 to 25 sec [25 to 35 sec].

Mini Main Dishes

Ham Quiche

1 Serving	[2 Servings]
Cornmeal Quiche Shell (right)	Cornmeal Quiche Shells (right)
3 tbsp shredded mozzarella cheese	1/3 cup shredded mozzarella cheese
1 1/2 tsp finely chopped green onion (with top)	1 tbsp finely chopped green onion (with top)
1 egg	2 eggs
3 tbsp milk	1/3 cup milk
1/8 tsp salt	1/4 tsp salt
3 drops red pepper sauce	6 drops red pepper sauce
1 tbsp finely chopped fully cooked smoked ham	2 tbsp finely chopped fully cooked smoked ham

Microwave Cornmeal Quiche Shell[s]. Sprinkle cheese and onion in shell[s]. Beat egg[s], milk, salt and pepper sauce with fork in 2-cup measure; stir in ham. Microwave uncovered on medium-high (385 watts) until warm, 1 to 1½ min [2 to 3 min, stirring after 1 min]. Stir; pour into shell[s]. Place shell[s] on inverted saucer[s] in microwave oven. Microwave uncovered on medium-high (385 watts) 2 min; turn dish[es] ½ turn. Microwave uncovered until center is almost set, 1 to 2 min [2 to 3 min].

Cover loosely and let stand on flat, heatproof surface 3 min.

Cornmeal Quiche Shell[s]

3 tbsp all-purpose flour	1/3 cup all-purpose flour
2 tsp cornmeal	
Dash of salt	1 tbsp plus 1 tsp cornmeal
1 tbsp shortening	1/8 tsp salt
2 1/2 to 3 tsp water	1 tbsp plus 2 tsp shortening
	5 to 6 tsp water

Mix flour, cornmeal and salt; cut in shortening thoroughly. Sprinkle in water, tossing with fork until all flour is moistened and pastry cleans side of bowl. Gather pastry into a ball. [Divide into halves.] Press pastry [each half] firmly against bottom and side of 10-oz quiche dish or custard cup [two 10-oz quiche dishes or custard cups]. Prick bottom and side thoroughly with fork. Place dish[es] on inverted saucer[s] in microwave oven. Microwave uncovered on high (550 watts) 1 min [2 min]; rotate dish[es] ½ turn. Prick any bubbles with fork. Microwave uncovered until pastry appears dry and flaky, 1 to 2 min [1½ to 3 min].

Ham Quiche

Scrambled Eggs

1 Serving	[2 Servings]
1½ tsp margarine or butter	1 tbsp margarine or butter
2 eggs	4 eggs
2 tbsp milk	¼ cup milk
⅛ tsp salt	¼ tsp salt
Dash of pepper	⅛ tsp pepper

Place margarine in 2-cup measure [1-qt measure]. Microwave uncovered on high (550 watts) until melted, 20 to 50 sec [45 sec to 1½ min]. Beat in remaining ingredients with fork. Microwave uncovered, stirring every min, until eggs are puffy and set but still moist, 1½ to 2½ min [2 to 4 min]. Stir before serving.

Mexican-style Egg

1 Serving	[2 Servings]
1 egg	2 eggs
1 tsp all-purpose flour	2 tsp all-purpose flour
1 tbsp milk	2 tbsp milk
¼ cup shredded Monterey Jack cheese	½ cup shredded Monterey Jack cheese
1 tbsp chopped green chilies, drained	2 tbsp chopped green chilies, drained
1 tbsp chopped ripe olives	2 tbsp chopped ripe olives
⅛ tsp salt	¼ tsp salt
⅛ tsp dried oregano leaves	¼ tsp dried oregano leaves

Beat egg[s], flour and milk with fork in 1-cup measure [2-cup measure]; stir in remaining ingredients. Pour into 12-oz shallow casserole [22-oz shallow casserole]. Cover with waxed paper and microwave on medium (275 watts), stirring every min, until set but still moist, 2½ to 4 min [5 to 8 min]. Serve with salsa if desired.

Egg and Potato Brunch Casserole

1 Serving	[2 Servings]
1½ tsp margarine or butter	1 tbsp margarine or butter
½ cup diced potatoes	1 cup diced potatoes
¼ cup chopped fully cooked smoked ham	½ cup chopped fully cooked smoked ham
½ medium tomato, chopped	1 medium tomato, chopped
1 green onion (with top), chopped	2 green onions (with tops), chopped
⅛ tsp salt	¼ tsp salt
Dash of pepper	⅛ tsp pepper
1 egg	2 eggs

Place margarine in 12-oz shallow casserole [two 12-oz shallow casseroles]. Microwave uncovered on high (550 watts) until melted, about 30 sec [about 45 sec]. Stir in potatoes, ham, tomato, onion[s], salt and pepper. Cover with vented plastic wrap and microwave until potatoes are tender, 3 to 5 min [5 to 8 min].

Make indentation[s] in center of mixture by pressing with back of spoon. Break egg[s] into indentation[s]; prick yolk[s] with wooden pick.

Cover and microwave on medium-high (385 watts) until egg is set or desired doneness, 2½ to 3½ min [3 to 5 min]. Garnish with parsley if desired.

Egg Benedict

1 Serving	[2 Servings]
Hollandaise Sauce (below)	*Hollandaise Sauce (below)*
2 slices Canadian-style bacon (1/8" thick)	4 slices Canadian-style bacon (1/8" thick)
2 tbsp hot water	1/4 cup hot water
1/4 tsp vinegar	1/2 tsp vinegar
1 egg	2 eggs
1/2 English muffin, toasted	1 English muffin, split and toasted

Prepare Hollandaise sauce. Place Canadian-style bacon on plate. Cover with waxed paper and microwave on high (550 watts) until hot, 30 to 60 sec **[45 to 60 sec]**.

Place water and vinegar in 6-oz custard cup [**divide water and vinegar between two 6-oz custard cups**]. Cover tightly and microwave on high (550 watts) until boiling, 20 to 30 sec [**30 to 60 sec**]. Break egg[**s**] into cup[**s**]; pierce yolk[**s**] with wooden pick. Cover tightly and microwave on medium (275 watts) until desired doneness, 45 sec to 1½ min [**1½ to 2½ min**]; drain.

Place English muffin half [**halves**] on plate[**s**]; top with Canadian-style bacon and egg[**s**]. Spoon Hollandaise Sauce over egg[**s**].

Hollandaise Sauce

1 Serving	[2 Servings]
Prepare Hollandaise Sauce for 2 servings. Reheat half of sauce to serve on vegetables.	3 tbsp margarine or butter
	1 tbsp lemon juice
	1 tbsp plus 1 tsp water
	1 egg yolk

Place margarine in 1-cup measure. Microwave uncovered on high (550 watts) just until melted, 30 to 45 sec. Add lemon juice and water. Beat in egg yolk with fork. Microwave uncovered on medium (275 watts), stirring every 15 sec, until thickened, 45 sec to 1½ min. Do not overmicrowave or sauce will curdle. Cover and let stand 3 min. Sauce will thicken as it stands. Refrigerate any remaining sauce.

Tip: To reheat sauce, cover tightly and microwave on medium (275 watts), stirring every 15 sec, until hot, 45 to 60 sec.

Eggs Benedict

Cheesy Omelet

1 Serving	[2 Servings]
1 egg, separated	2 eggs, separated
2 tsp water	1 tbsp water
1½ tsp mayonnaise or salad dressing	1 tbsp mayonnaise or salad dressing
Dash of salt	⅛ tsp salt
Dash of pepper	⅛ tsp pepper
1 tsp margarine or butter	2 tsp margarine or butter
2 tbsp shredded Cheddar cheese	¼ cup shredded Cheddar cheese
1½ tsp imitation bacon	1 tbsp imitation bacon
1 chopped green onion (with top)	2 chopped green onions (with tops)

Beat egg white[s] with hand beater until stiff but not dry. Beat egg yolk[s], water, mayonnaise, salt and pepper until slightly thick and lemon-colored. Fold into egg white[s].

Place margarine in 16-oz shallow casserole [two **16-oz shallow casseroles**], 6¾" in diameter. Microwave uncovered on high (550 watts) until melted, 30 to 60 sec [**45 to 60 sec**]. Tilt casserole[s] to coat with margarine. Pour egg mixture into casserole[s]. Microwave uncovered on medium (275 watts) until puffy and set but still moist, 2 to 3½ min [**6 to 9 min, rearranging casseroles after 4 min**]. Sprinkle with cheese and bacon. Run spatula under omelet[s] to loosen; fold in half. Slip onto warm plate[s]. Sprinkle with onion[s].

Crabmeat Quiche

1 Serving	[2 Servings]
Cornmeal Quiche Shell (page 65)	Cornmeal Quiche Shells (page 65)
2 tbsp shredded Swiss cheese	¼ cup shredded Swiss cheese
1 tsp snipped chives	2 tsp snipped chives
1 egg	2 eggs
3 tbsp milk	⅓ cup milk
⅛ tsp salt	¼ tsp salt
Freshly ground pepper	Freshly ground pepper
2 tbsp cooked crabmeat	¼ cup cooked crabmeat

Microwave Cornmeal Quiche Shell[s]. Sprinkle cheese and chives in shell[s]. Beat egg[s], milk, salt and pepper in 2-cup measure; stir in crabmeat. Microwave uncovered on medium-high (385 watts) until warm, 1 to 1½ min [**2 to 3 min, stirring after 1 min**]. Stir; pour into shell[s]. Place shell[s] on inverted saucer[s] in microwave oven. Microwave uncovered on medium-high (385 watts) 2 min; turn dish[es] ½ turn. Microwave uncovered until center is almost set, 1 to 2 min [**2 to 3 min**]. Cover loosely and let stand on flat, heatproof surface 3 min.

Cheesy Omelet

English Muffin Pizza

1 Serving	[2 Servings]
⅛ lb bulk Italian sausage (⅓ cup)	¼ lb bulk Italian sausage (⅔ cup)
1 English muffin, split and toasted	2 English muffins, split and toasted
2 tbsp pizza sauce	¼ cup pizza sauce
1 tbsp chopped green pepper	2 tbsp chopped green pepper
2 tbsp shredded mozzarella cheese	¼ cup shredded mozzarella cheese
1 tsp grated Parmesan cheese	2 tsp grated Parmesan cheese

Crumble bulk Italian sausage into 10-oz custard cup [15-oz casserole]. Cover loosely and microwave on high (550 watts), stirring every min, until done, 2 to 3 min [3 to 4 min]; break up and drain.

Spread 1 tbsp pizza sauce over each English muffin half. Top with sausage and remaining ingredients. Place on plate. Microwave uncovered on high (550 watts) until cheese is melted and bubbly, 1 to 2 min [2 to 3 min].

Macaroni and Cheese

1 Serving	[2 Servings]
½ cup uncooked macaroni	1 cup uncooked macaroni
½ cup hot water	1 cup hot water
1 tbsp chopped green onion (with top)	2 tbsp chopped green onion (with top)
1 tbsp margarine or butter	2 tbsp margarine or butter
⅛ tsp salt	¼ tsp salt
⅛ tsp dry mustard	¼ tsp dry mustard
Dash of pepper	⅛ tsp pepper
½ cup shredded sharp American cheese	1 cup shredded sharp American cheese
⅓ cup milk	⅔ cup milk
1 tbsp all-purpose flour	2 tbsp all-purpose flour

Mix macaroni, water, onion, margarine, salt, mustard and pepper in 24-oz casserole [1½-qt casserole]. Cover with vented plastic wrap and microwave on high (550 watts) 2 min [3 min]; stir. Cover with vented plastic wrap and microwave on medium (275 watts) until boiling, 1 to 2 min longer [2 to 3 min longer]. Stir in remaining ingredients. Cover with vented plastic wrap and microwave on high (550 watts), stirring every min, until mixture is bubbly and macaroni is tender, 2 to 3 min [3 to 4 min]. Sprinkle with paprika if desired.

Cheese Enchiladas

1 Serving	[2 Servings]
¼ cup creamed cottage cheese (small curd)	½ cup creamed cottage cheese (small curd)
¼ cup shredded Monterey Jack cheese	½ cup shredded Monterey Jack cheese
¼ cup chopped tomatoes	½ cup chopped tomatoes
2 tbsp sliced green onion (with top)	¼ cup sliced green onions (with top)
½ tsp chili powder	1 tsp chili powder
⅛ tsp salt	¼ tsp salt
½ small clove garlic, finely chopped	1 small clove garlic, finely chopped
Two 6" corn tortillas	Four 6" corn tortillas
2 tbsp mild taco sauce	¼ cup mild taco sauce
2 tbsp shredded Monterey Jack cheese	¼ cup shredded Monterey Jack cheese

Mix cottage cheese, ¼ cup [½ cup] Monterey Jack cheese, the tomatoes, onion[s], chili powder, salt and garlic; reserve.

Place tortillas in 1 stack [2 stacks] on plate[s]. Cover with waxed paper and microwave on medium (275 watts) until softened, 20 to 30 sec [30 to 40 sec]. Spoon about ⅓ cup of the cheese mixture onto each tortilla. Roll tortillas around cheese mixture. Arrange tortillas, seam sides down, in 14-oz shallow casserole [two 14-oz shallow casseroles].

Spoon taco sauce over tortilla[s]. Cover with vented plastic wrap and microwave on medium-high (385 watts) until hot, 2 to 3 min [3 to 4 min]. Sprinkle with 2 tbsp [¼ cup] Monterey Jack cheese. Microwave uncovered on high (550 watts) until cheese is melted, 30 to 40 sec [45 to 60 sec]. Top with sliced ripe olives if desired.

Cheese Enchiladas

Steak Burger

1 Serving	[2 Servings]
¼ lb ground beef	*½ lb ground beef*
1 tsp steak sauce	*2 tsp steak sauce*
½ tsp Dijon-style mustard	*1 tsp Dijon-style mustard*
⅛ tsp onion powder	*¼ tsp onion powder*
Dash of salt	*⅛ tsp salt*
Dash of pepper	*⅛ tsp pepper*
2 mushrooms, sliced	*4 mushrooms, sliced*
1 hard roll, split and toasted	*2 hard rolls, split and toasted*

Mix ground beef, steak sauce, mustard, onion powder, salt and pepper. Shape into patty [**2 patties**], about ¾" thick. Arrange mushrooms in circle [**2 circles**] on rack in 11 × 7 × 1½" dish; place patty [**patties**] on mushrooms. Cover with waxed paper and microwave on high (550 watts) until almost done, 2 to 3 min [**3 to 4 min**]. Serve on hard roll[**s**] with mushrooms on top.

Welsh Rabbit

1 Serving	[2 Servings]
1 tbsp margarine or butter	*2 tbsp margarine or butter*
1 tbsp all-purpose flour	*2 tbsp all-purpose flour*
⅛ tsp salt	*¼ tsp salt*
Dash of dry mustard	*⅛ tsp dry mustard*
¼ cup milk	*½ cup milk*
2 tbsp dry white wine	*¼ cup dry white wine*
¼ cup shredded sharp Cheddar cheese	*½ cup shredded sharp Cheddar cheese*
Two 1" slices French bread, toasted	*Four 1" slices French bread, toasted*

Place margarine in 2-cup measure [**4-cup measure**]. Microwave uncovered on high (550 watts) until melted, 20 to 45 sec [**45 to 60 sec**]. Mix in flour, salt and mustard. Gradually stir in milk. Microwave uncovered, stirring every 30 sec, until boiling, 1 to 1½ min [**1½ to 2 min**]. Stir in wine and cheese. Microwave uncovered 30 sec [**45 sec**]; stir. Microwave uncovered until cheese is melted, 15 to 60 sec longer [**15 to 45 sec longer**]. Serve over French bread.

Cheese-stuffed Manicotti

1 Serving	[**2 Servings**]
½ cup spaghetti sauce	**1 cup spaghetti sauce**
¼ cup shredded mozzarella cheese	**½ cup shredded mozzarella cheese**
¼ cup ricotta cheese	**½ cup ricotta cheese**
2 tbsp grated Parmesan cheese	**¼ cup grated Parmesan cheese**
½ small clove garlic, finely chopped	**1 small clove garlic, finely chopped**
Freshly ground pepper	**Freshly ground pepper**
3 manicotti tubes, cooked, drained and cooled	**6 manicotti tubes, cooked, drained and cooled**

Spread 2 tbsp of the spaghetti sauce in 24-oz shallow casserole [**2 tbsp in each of two 24-oz shallow casseroles**]. Mix remaining ingredients except manicotti tubes and remaining spaghetti sauce. Fill each manicotti tube with about 2 tbsp cheese mixture; arrange in casserole[**s**]. Spoon remaining spaghetti sauce over tops, covering manicotti tubes completely. Cover with vented plastic wrap and microwave on medium-high (385 watts) until hot, 3 to 5 min [**6 to 8 min**].

Savory Beef Hoagie

1 Serving	[**2 Servings**]
¼ lb ground beef	**½ lb ground beef**
2 tbsp chopped onion	**¼ cup chopped onion**
1 tbsp chopped green pepper	**2 tbsp chopped green pepper**
2 tbsp chili sauce	**¼ cup chili sauce**
1 tbsp dry red wine	**2 tbsp dry red wine**
⅛ tsp salt	**¼ tsp salt**
3 drops red pepper sauce	**6 drops red pepper sauce**
1 hoagie bun	**2 hoagie buns**

Crumble ground beef into 2-cup measure [**4-cup measure**]. Add onion and green pepper. Cover loosely and microwave on high (550 watts) until very little pink remains, 1 to 1¼ min [**1½ to 2 min**]; break up and drain. Stir in remaining ingredients except bun[**s**]. Cover tightly and microwave until hot, 1 to 1½ min [**1½ to 2 min**]; stir. Fill bun[**s**] with beef mixture.

Corned Beef Sandwich

1 Serving	[2 Servings]
½ tsp margarine or butter, softened	1 tsp margarine or butter, softened
¼ tsp prepared mustard	½ tsp prepared mustard
¼ tsp prepared horseradish	½ tsp prepared horseradish
1 slice dark rye bread, toasted	2 slices dark rye bread, toasted
1 oz thinly sliced cooked corned beef	2 oz thinly sliced cooked corned beef
2 thin slices avocado	4 thin slices avocado
1 slice mozzarella cheese	2 slices mozzarella cheese

Mix margarine, mustard and horseradish; spread over toast. Arrange corned beef and avocado on toast; top with cheese. Place on rack in 11 × 7 × 1½" dish. Microwave uncovered on medium-high (385 watts) until cheese is melted, 45 sec to 1½ min [**1½ to 2¼ min**].

Blue Cheese Burger

1 Serving	[2 Servings]
¼ lb ground beef	½ lb ground beef
1 tbsp blue cheese, crumbled	2 tbsp blue cheese, crumbled
⅛ tsp onion powder	¼ tsp onion powder
⅛ tsp salt	¼ tsp salt
Dash of pepper	⅛ tsp pepper
⅛ tsp browning sauce	¼ tsp browning sauce
⅛ tsp water	¼ tsp water
1 English muffin, split and toasted	2 English muffins, split and toasted
1 tbsp blue cheese dressing	2 tbsp blue cheese dressing
1 pimiento-stuffed olive, sliced	2 pimiento-stuffed olives, sliced

Mix ground beef, cheese, onion powder, salt and pepper. Shape into patty [**2 patties**], about ¾" thick. Mix browning sauce and water; brush over both sides of patty [**patties**]. Place on rack in 11 × 7 × 1½" dish. Cover with waxed paper and microwave on high (550 watts) until almost done, 2 to 3 min [**3 to 4 min**]. Place on bottom[**s**] of English muffin[**s**]. Top with salad dressing, olive[**s**] and top[**s**] of English muffin[**s**].

Corned Beef Sandwich

Tuna Salad Croissant

1 Serving	[2 Servings]
½ can (6½-oz size) tuna, drained	1 can (6½ oz) tuna, drained
1 tbsp chopped green onion (with top)	2 tbsp chopped green onion (with top)
1 tbsp mayonnaise or salad dressing	2 tbsp mayonnaise or salad dressing
1 tsp lemon juice	2 tsp lemon juice
Dash of pepper	⅛ tsp pepper
1 large croissant, cut lengthwise into halves	2 large croissants, cut lengthwise into halves
¼ cup alfalfa sprouts	½ cup alfalfa sprouts

Mix all ingredients except croissant[**s**] and alfalfa sprouts in 2-cup measure [**4-cup measure**]. Cover with waxed paper and microwave on high (550 watts) until hot, 1 to 1½ min [**2½ to 3 min**]. Spread tuna mixture over bottom[**s**] of croissant[**s**]; top with alfalfa sprouts. Replace top[**s**] of croissant[**s**].

Tacos

1 Serving	[2 Servings]
¼ cup shredded cooked beef, pork or chicken	½ cup shredded cooked beef, pork or chicken
1 tbsp finely chopped green onion (with top)	2 tbsp finely chopped green onion (with top)
⅛ tsp salt	¼ tsp salt
Dash of crushed red peppers, if desired	Dash of crushed red peppers, if desired
½ small clove garlic, finely chopped	1 small clove garlic, finely chopped
¼ cup chopped tomato	½ cup chopped tomato
2 taco shells	4 taco shells
Shredded lettuce	Shredded lettuce
Shredded Cheddar cheese	Shredded Cheddar cheese
Taco sauce	Taco sauce

Mix beef, onion, salt, red peppers and garlic in 2-cup measure [**4-cup measure**]. Cover tightly and microwave on high (550 watts) until beef is hot, 1 to 1½ min [**1½ to 2 min**]. Stir in tomatoes. Spoon into taco shells; place in 7 × 4¾ × 1" baking dish [**two 7 × 4¾ × 1" baking dishes**]. Microwave uncovered on high (550 watts) until filling is hot, 30 to 60 sec [**1 to 1½ min**]. Serve with lettuce, cheese and taco sauce and, if desired, with sour cream.

Burritos

1 Serving	[2 Servings]
¼ lb bulk pork sausage	½ lb bulk pork sausage
¼ cup jalapeño bean dip	½ cup jalapeño bean dip
1 tbsp taco sauce	2 tbsp taco sauce
¼ to ½ tsp chili powder	½ to 1 tsp chili powder
½ small clove garlic,	1 small clove garlic,
finely chopped	finely chopped
Dash of salt	⅛ tsp salt
Two 6" flour tortillas	Four 6" flour tortillas
¼ cup shredded Cheddar	½ cup shredded Cheddar cheese
cheese	

Crumble pork sausage into 2-cup measure [**4-cup measure**]. Cover loosely and microwave on high (550 watts) until very little pink remains, 1½ to 2 min [**2 to 2½ min**]; break up and drain. Stir in bean dip, taco sauce, chili powder, garlic and salt. Cover loosely and microwave on high (550 watts) until hot and bubbly, 1¼ to 2 min [**2 to 3½ min**]; stir.

Wrap tortillas in damp cloth and microwave on high (550 watts) until softened, 30 to 45 sec [**1 to 2 min**]. Spread about ⅓ cup filling on each tortilla (keep remaining tortilla[**s**] covered to prevent them from drying out); sprinkle with 2 tbsp cheese. Fold up bottom of tortilla. Fold sides over and roll from bottom. Arrange burritos, seam sides down, in 22-oz shallow casserole [**two 22-oz shallow casseroles**]. Cover loosely and microwave on high (550 watts) until hot, 1¼ to 2 min [**2½ to 3½ min**]. Serve with taco sauce if desired.

Tostada

1 Serving	[2 Servings]
1 tsp margarine or	2 tsp margarine or
butter	butter
¼ tsp cornstarch	½ tsp cornstarch
1 tbsp chopped green	2 tbsp chopped green
pepper	pepper
2 tsp finely chopped	1 tbsp finely chopped
onion	onion
Dash of garlic powder	⅛ tsp garlic powder
Dash of ground	⅛ tsp ground cumin
cumin	½ cup shredded cooked
¼ cup shredded cooked	pork or beef
pork or beef	⅓ cup chopped tomato
3 tbsp chopped tomato	¼ tsp salt
⅛ tsp salt	2 tostada shells
1 tostada shell	¼ cup shredded
2 tbsp shredded	Monterey Jack
Monterey Jack cheese	cheese

Place margarine in 2-cup measure [**4-cup measure**]. Microwave uncovered on high (550 watts) until melted, 15 to 20 sec [**20 to 30 sec**]. Mix in cornstarch. Stir in green pepper, onion, garlic powder and cumin. Cover tightly and microwave on high (550 watts) until vegetables are hot, 45 to 60 sec [**1 to 1½ min**]. Stir in beef, tomato and salt. Cover tightly and microwave until beef is hot, 1 to 1½ min [**1½ to 1¾ min**].

Place tostada shell[**s**] on plate[**s**]; top with beef mixture and shredded cheese. Serve with shredded lettuce, dairy sour cream and salsa if desired.

Hero Sandwich

1 Serving	[2 Servings]
6" piece French bread, cut lengthwise into halves	*Two 6" pieces French bread, cut lengthwise into halves*
1 tbsp margarine or butter, softened	*2 tbsp margarine or butter, softened*
⅛ tsp Italian seasoning Dash of garlic powder	*¼ tsp Italian seasoning*
4 thin slices green pepper	*⅛ tsp garlic powder*
1 oz thinly sliced salami	*8 thin slices green pepper*
1 thin slice onion, separated into rings	*2 oz thinly sliced salami*
½ oz thinly sliced fully cooked smoked ham	*2 thin slices onion, separated into rings*
3 thin slices tomato	*1 oz thinly sliced fully cooked smoked ham*
2 slices process American cheese, cut diagonally into halves	*6 thin slices tomato*
	4 slices process American cheese, cut diagonally into halves

Spread cut surface[s] of bread with margarine; sprinkle with Italian seasoning and garlic powder. Arrange remaining ingredients except cheese on bottom portion[s] of bread; place on plate[s]. Cover with waxed paper and microwave on high (550 watts) until warm, 1 to 1½ min [1½ to 2 min]. Add cheese and top portion[s] of bread. Microwave uncovered until cheese is slightly melted, 30 to 60 sec [1 to 1½ min]. Serve with pimiento-stuffed olives and ripe olives if desired.

Hero Sandwich

Frank in Bun Special

Frank in Bun Special

1 Serving	**[2 Servings]**
1 frankfurter	*2 frankfurters*
1 hot dog bun	*2 hot dog buns*
Prepared mustard	*Prepared mustard*
2 tbsp well-drained sauerkraut or coleslaw	*¼ cup well-drained sauerkraut or coleslaw*
2 tbsp shredded Cheddar cheese	*¼ cup shredded Cheddar cheese*

Split frankfurter[s] lengthwise, not cutting completely through. Place bun[s] on piece[s] of waxed paper large enough to wrap bun[s] and secure by twisting both ends. Spread mustard on bun[s]. Place frankfurter[s] in bun[s]. Fill with sauerkraut; sprinkle with cheese. Wrap in waxed paper; twist ends. Place frankfurter[s], split side[s] up, on plate. Microwave on high (550 watts) until cheese is melted, 1 to 1½ min **[2 to 2½ min]**. Unwrap and serve immediately.

Pocket Sandwich

1 Serving	**[2 Servings]**
2 tbsp chopped avocado	*¼ cup chopped avocado*
½ tsp lemon juice	*1 tsp lemon juice*
½ cup finely cut-up lean cooked lamb	*1 cup finely cut-up lean cooked lamb*
2 tbsp chopped tomato	*¼ cup chopped tomato*
1 tbsp chopped green onion (with top)	*2 tbsp chopped green onion (with top)*
½ tsp snipped mint leaves or ¼ tsp dried mint leaves	*1 tsp snipped mint leaves or ½ tsp dried mint leaves*
¼ tsp salt	*½ tsp salt*
Freshly ground pepper	*Freshly ground pepper*
1 pita bread (5" in diameter)	*2 pita breads (5" in diameter)*
Plain yogurt	*Plain yogurt*

Sprinkle avocado with lemon juice; reserve. Mix remaining ingredients except pita bread[s] and yogurt in 2-cup measure **[4-cup measure]**. Cover loosely and microwave on high (550 watts) until hot, 1½ to 2 min **[2 to 3 min]**; stir. Slit pita bread[s] halfway through to form pocket[s]. Fill with lamb mixture. Top with avocado and serve with yogurt.

79

Curried Shrimp Soup

1 Serving	[2 Servings]
½ can (4½-oz size) broken shrimp, rinsed and drained	1 can (4½ oz) broken shrimp, rinsed and drained
1 cup hot water	2 cups hot water
1 tsp instant chicken bouillon	2 tsp instant chicken bouillon
½ tsp curry powder	1 tsp curry powder
Dash of pepper	Dash of pepper
Snipped parsley	Snipped parsley

Mix all ingredients except parsley in 2-cup measure [**4-cup measure**]. Microwave uncovered on high (550 watts) until boiling, 2 to 2½ min [**3 to 4 min**]. Sprinkle with parsley.

Zucchini Soup

1 Serving	[2 Servings]
1 slice bacon, cut into ½" pieces	2 slices bacon, cut into ½" pieces
¾ cup milk	1½ cups milk
¼ cup hot water	½ cup hot water
1½ tsp finely chopped onion	1 tbsp finely chopped onion
1 tsp instant chicken bouillon	2 tsp instant chicken bouillon
4 drops red pepper sauce	8 drops red pepper sauce
¼ cup shredded zucchini	½ cup shredded zucchini

Place bacon in 2-cup measure [**4-cup measure**]. Cover loosely and microwave on high (550 watts) until almost crisp, 1½ to 2 min [**2½ to 3 min**]. Remove bacon with slotted spoon; crumble and reserve. Stir remaining ingredients except zucchini into bacon fat. Cover tightly and microwave until boiling, 1½ to 2 min [**2 to 2½ min**]. Stir in zucchini. Microwave uncovered until hot, 30 to 60 sec [**1 to 1½ min**]. Sprinkle with bacon.

Cheese Soup

1 Serving	[2 Servings]
2 tbsp water	¼ cup water
1 tbsp finely chopped celery	2 tbsp finely chopped celery
1 tsp finely chopped onion	2 tsp finely chopped onion
1 tbsp margarine or butter	2 tbsp margarine or butter
1 tbsp all-purpose flour	2 tbsp all-purpose flour
¾ cup milk	1½ cups milk
1 tsp instant chicken bouillon	2 tsp instant chicken bouillon
⅛ tsp paprika	¼ tsp paprika
¼ cup shredded sharp process American cheese	½ cup shredded sharp process American cheese

Place water, celery and onion in 1-cup measure. Cover tightly and microwave on high (550 watts) until tender, 1 to 1½ min [**1½ to 2 min**]; reserve.

Place margarine in 2-cup measure [**4-cup measure**]. Microwave uncovered on high (550 watts) until melted, 20 to 30 sec [**45 to 60 sec**]. Mix in flour. Stir in celery and onion, milk, bouillon (dry) and paprika. Microwave uncovered until boiling, 1½ to 2 min [**2½ to 3½ min**]. Stir in cheese. Microwave uncovered on medium-high (385 watts) until melted, 1 to 1½ min [**1½ to 2 min**]; stir. Garnish with popcorn if desired.

Green Pea Soup

1 Serving	[2 Servings]
1 slice bacon, cut into ½" pieces	2 slices bacon, cut into ½" pieces
½ cup frozen green peas	1 cup frozen green peas
½ cup hot water	1 cup hot water
1 tsp instant chicken bouillon	2 tsp instant chicken bouillon
¼ tsp instant minced onion	½ tsp instant minced onion
Dash of dried marjoram leaves	Dash of dried marjoram leaves
Dash of pepper	Dash of pepper
½ cup half-and-half	1 cup half-and-half

Place bacon in 2-cup measure [**4-cup measure**]. Cover loosely and microwave on high (550 watts) until almost crisp, 1½ to 2 min [**2½ to 3 min**]. Stir in peas, water, bouillon (dry), onion, marjoram and pepper. Cover tightly and microwave until peas are tender, 4 to 5 min [**6 to 7 min**]. Mash peas with fork; stir in half-and-half. Microwave uncovered until hot, 1 to 1½ min [**1½ to 2 min**]. Sprinkle with croutons if desired.

Fresh Mushroom Soup

1 Serving	[2 Servings]
1 tbsp chopped green onion (with top)	2 tbsp chopped green onion (with top)
1½ tsp margarine	1 tbsp margarine
1½ tsp flour	1 tbsp flour
¾ cup hot water	1½ cups hot water
½ cup sliced mushrooms	1 cup sliced mushrooms
1 tsp instant chicken bouillon	2 tsp instant chicken bouillon
Dash of white pepper	Dash of white pepper
¼ cup half-and-half	½ cup half-and-half

Place onion and margarine in 2-cup measure [**4-cup measure**]. Cover tightly and microwave on high (550 watts) until onion is tender, 1 to 1½ min [**1½ to 2 min**]. Mix in flour. Stir in water, mushrooms, bouillon (dry) and pepper. Cover tightly and microwave until boiling, 1½ to 2 min [**2 to 2½ min**]. Stir in half-and-half. Microwave uncovered until hot, 30 to 60 sec [**1 to 1½ min**].

Green Pea Soup

French Onion Soup

1 Serving	[2 Servings]
½ cup thinly sliced onions	1 cup thinly sliced onions
1½ tsp margarine or butter	1 tbsp margarine or butter
1 cup hot water	2 cups hot water
1½ tsp instant beef bouillon	1 tbsp instant beef bouillon
Freshly ground pepper	Freshly ground pepper
1" slice French bread, toasted	Two 1" slices French bread, toasted
¼ cup shredded mozzarella cheese	½ cup shredded mozzarella cheese
1 tsp grated Parmesan cheese	2 tsp grated Parmesan cheese

Separate onions into rings. Place onions and margarine in 12-oz bowl [**two 12-oz bowls**]. Cover tightly and microwave on high (550 watts) until tender, 2 to 3 min [**4 to 5 min**]. Stir in water, bouillon and pepper. Cover tightly and microwave until boiling, 1½ to 2½ min [**4 to 5 min**]. Place toast on top[**s**]. Mix cheeses; sprinkle over toast. Microwave uncovered on medium-high (385 watts) until cheese is melted, 1 to 2 min [**2½ to 3 min**].

Beet Soup

1 Serving	[2 Servings]
¾ cup hot water	1½ cups hot water
½ tsp instant beef bouillon	1 tsp instant beef bouillon
½ can (8¼-oz size) diced beets, undrained	1 can (8¼ oz) diced beets, undrained
1 tbsp dry white wine	2 tbsp dry white wine
⅛ tsp salt	¼ tsp salt
Dash of dried dill weed	Dash of dried dill weed
Freshly ground pepper	Freshly ground pepper
Dairy sour cream	Dairy sour cream

Mix water and bouillon (dry) in 2-cup measure [**4-cup measure**]. Stir in remaining ingredients except sour cream. Microwave uncovered on high (550 watts) until hot, 3 to 4 min [**5 to 6 min**]; stir. Top with spoonful of sour cream.

Vegetable-Beef Soup

1 Serving	[2 Servings]
⅓ cup hot water	½ cup hot water
¼ cup ⅛" slices carrot ⅛" slice medium onion, separated into rings	½ cup ⅛" slices carrot Two ⅛" slices medium onion, separated into rings
⅓ cup hot water	¾ cup hot water
¼ cup shredded cooked beef	½ cup shredded cooked beef
¼ cup shredded lettuce	½ cup shredded lettuce
⅛ tsp salt	¼ tsp salt
⅛ tsp browning sauce	¼ tsp browning sauce
Dash of pepper	⅛ tsp pepper
Dash of dried basil leaves	⅛ tsp dried basil leaves
½ can (8-oz size) whole tomatoes, undrained, cut up	1 can (8 oz) whole tomatoes, undrained, cut up

Place ⅓ cup hot water [**½ cup hot water**], the carrot and onion in 1-qt casserole [**1½-qt casserole**]. Cover tightly and microwave on high (550 watts) until carrot is tender, 2 to 3 min [**2½ to 3½ min**]. Stir in ⅓ cup hot water [**¾ cup hot water**] and the remaining ingredients. Cover tightly and microwave until boiling, 4 to 5 min [**6 to 8 min**].

Chicken and Ham Soup

1 Serving	[2 Servings]
¾ cup hot water	1½ cups hot water
¼ cup cut-up cooked chicken	½ cup cut-up cooked chicken
2 tbsp cut-up fully cooked smoked ham	¼ cup cut-up fully cooked smoked ham
2 tbsp uncooked instant rice	¼ cup uncooked instant rice
1 tsp instant chicken bouillon	2 tsp instant chicken bouillon
⅛ tsp onion powder	¼ tsp onion powder
Dash of pepper	⅛ tsp pepper
½ can (8-oz size) stewed tomatoes	1 can (8 oz) stewed tomatoes

Mix all ingredients in 1-qt casserole [**1½-qt casserole**]. Cover tightly and microwave on high (550 watts) until boiling, 4 to 5 min [**8 to 9 min**]. Let stand covered 3 min [**4 min**].

Reheating Main Dishes

Many main dishes reheat well in the microwave. For fastest heating and to prevent spattering, cover food as directed below. If a casserole contains delicate foods such as eggs or cheese, or contains large pieces of meat, a lower power level setting than listed will help avoid overcooking.

| Type of Main Dish | Amount | | Power Level Setting | Procedure | Time |
	1 Serving	[2 Servings]			
Chicken pieces, cooked	3 oz	6 oz	medium-high (385 watts)	cover with waxed paper	45 sec to 2 min [1 to 3½ min]
Frankfurters or sausage, fully cooked	2 to 4 oz	4 to 8 oz	high (550 watts)	cover with waxed paper	20 sec to 1½ min [30 sec to 2½ min]
Meat loaf or hamburgers, cooked	3 to 4 oz	6 to 8 oz	high (550 watts)	cover tightly	45 sec to 2 min [1 to 3 min]
Meat, roasted and thinly sliced with gravy or sauce	3 oz	6 oz	medium-high (385 watts)	cover with waxed paper	30 sec to 1¼ min [1 to 2½ min]
Meatballs in sauce, stew, spaghetti, lasagne, macaroni and cheese	1 cup	2 cups	medium-high (385 watts)	cover with waxed paper; stir once during microwaving	2 to 4 min [3½ to 7 min]
Pasta or rice, cooked	¾ to 1 cup	1½ to 2 cups	high (550 watts)	cover tightly	30 sec to 2¼ min [1 to 4 min]
Ribs, cooked	8 oz	1 lb	medium-high (385 watts)	uncovered	1½ to 4½ min [4 to 10 min]
Sandwiches (frozen bread with a refrigerated filling can also be micro-waved)	1	2	medium-high (385 watts)	cover with waxed paper and place on rack	1 to 3 min [1½ to 4 min]
Soup, milk based	1 cup	2 cups	medium-high (385 watts)	cover tightly	2 to 4 min [3½ to 5½ min]
Soup, water based	1 cup	2 cups	high (550 watts)	cover tightly	1 to 3 min [2½ to 6½ min]

Side Dishes

Microwaving Fresh Vegetables

Season vegetables, if desired, after microwaving. (Salt sprinkled on vegetables before microwaving causes shriveling.) For even cooking, do not crowd vegetables in utensils.

Vegetable	Amount 1 Serving	[2 Servings]	Microwave Procedure on High (550 Watts)
Artichokes, globe (whole)	1 (5 oz)	**2 (5 oz each)**	Cover artichoke[s] and ¼ to ½ cup water tightly and microwave 3 min; rotate dish ½ turn. Microwave until leaves pull out easily and bottom is tender when pierced with knife, 4½ to 5 min longer [**8½ to 10 min longer**]. Carefully remove artichoke[s]; place upside down to drain.
Asparagus (1" pieces)	½ cup	**1 cup**	Cover asparagus and 1 to 2 tsp water tightly and microwave until crisp-tender, 1½ to 2 min [**2½ to 3 min**]. Let stand 1 min; drain.
Asparagus (spears)	4 (2 oz)	**8 (4 oz)**	Arrange asparagus spears lengthwise in dish with tips in center. Add 1 to 2 tbsp water. Cover tightly and microwave 1 min; rotate dish ½ turn. Microwave until crisp-tender, 2 to 2½ min longer [**4 to 5 min longer**]. Let stand 1 min; drain.
Beans, green or wax (1" pieces)	½ cup	**1 cup**	Cover beans and 2 to 3 tbsp water tightly and microwave until tender, 2½ to 3½ min [**4 to 5 min**]. Let stand 2 min; drain.
Broccoli (1" pieces)	½ cup	**1 cup**	Cover broccoli and 1 to 2 tbsp water tightly and microwave until almost tender, 1½ to 2 min [**3½ to 4 min**]. Let stand 1 min; drain.
Broccoli (thin spears)	2 (1 oz)	**4 (2 oz)**	Arrange broccoli in dish with tips in center. Add 2 to 3 tsp water. Cover tightly and microwave 1 min; rotate dish ½ turn. Microwave until tender, 1½ to 2 min longer [**4 to 4½ min longer**]. Let stand 1 min; drain.

Microwaving Fresh Vegetables (continued)

Vegetable	Amount 1 Serving	[2 Servings]	Microwave Procedure on High (550 Watts)
Cabbage (shredded)	½ cup	1 cup	Cover cabbage and 1 to 2 tbsp water tightly and microwave until crisp-tender, 2 to 2½ min [3½ to 4 min]; drain.
Cabbage (wedges)	1 (4 oz)	2 (8 oz)	Cover cabbage and 1 to 2 tbsp water tightly and microwave 2 min; rotate dish ½ turn. Microwave until crisp-tender, 2 to 3 min longer [5 to 6 min longer]. Let stand 2 min; drain.
Carrots (¼" slices)	¾ cup	1½ cups	Cover carrots and 1 to 2 tbsp water tightly and microwave until tender, 3½ to 4 min [6½ to 7 min]; drain.
Cauliflower (flowerets)	½ cup	1 cup	Cover cauliflower and 1 to 2 tsp water tightly and microwave until tender, 1½ to 2 min [2½ to 3½ min].
Corn on the cob (ears)	1	2	Wrap each ear of husked corn in plastic wrap or waxed paper; twist ends. Microwave 2 min; turn corn over. Microwave until tender, 2 to 3 min longer [3 to 4 min longer]. Let stand 3 min.
Greens, spinach, beet tops or mustard	2 cups (1 oz)	4 cups (2 oz)	Rinse greens; shake off excess moisture. Cover tightly and microwave 1 min; stir. Microwave until tender, 30 to 60 sec longer [2 to 2½ min longer].
Mushrooms (sliced)	1 cup	2 cups	Cut mushrooms parallel to stem into ¼" slices. Cover mushrooms and 1 to 2 tsp margarine or butter tightly and microwave 30 sec; stir. Microwave until tender, 30 to 60 sec longer [2 to 2½ min longer].
Peas, green	½ cup	1 cup	Cover peas and 2 to 3 tsp water tightly and microwave until crisp-tender, 2½ to 3 min [4½ to 5 min]. Let stand 1 min; drain.
Potatoes, white or sweet (whole)	1	2	Prick potato[es] to allow steam to escape. Microwave 3 min; turn potatoes over. Microwave until tender when pierced with fork, 1½ to 2 min longer [2½ to 4 min longer]. Wrap potato[es] in aluminum foil; let stand 5 min.

Microwaving Fresh Vegetables (continued)

Vegetable	Amount		Microwave Procedure on High (550 Watts)
	1 Serving	[2 Servings]	
Squash, pattypan or zucchini (¼" slices)	1 cup	**2 cups**	Cover squash and 1 to 2 tsp water tightly and microwave 1 min; stir. Microwave until crisp-tender, 30 sec to 1½ min longer [**2 to 3 min longer**].
Squash, acorn (whole)	½	**1**	Prick whole squash to allow steam to escape. Microwave 2 min; carefully cut into halves and remove seeds. Place squash, cut side[**s**] down, in dish. Cover tightly and microwave 3 min; rotate dish ½ turn. Microwave until tender, 1½ to 2 min longer [**2 to 4 min longer**].

Microwaving Frozen Vegetables

Place frozen vegetables and 1 to 3 tsp water in 10-oz or 21-oz casserole. Cover tightly and microwave on high (550 watts), stirring once, for amount of time directed in chart below. Season vegetables, if desired, after microwaving or add salt to water in casserole before adding vegetables. (Salt sprinkled on vegetables before microwaving causes shriveling.)

Frozen vegetables purchased in 6- to 10-oz bag or box should be microwaved as directed on package.

Vegetable	Microwave Time on High (550 Watts)	
	1 Serving (½ cup)	[2 Servings] (1 cup)
Asparagus (cuts or spears)	1½ to 2 min	**3½ to 4 min**
Beans, green or wax (cuts)	2½ to 3 min	**4 to 4½ min**
Beans, lima	2 to 2½ min	**3½ to 4½ min**
Broccoli (cuts or spears)	2½ to 3 min	**3½ to 4 min**
Brussels sprouts	2½ to 3 min	**4 to 5 min**
Carrots (sliced)	2½ to 3 min	**4 to 4½ min**
Cauliflower (flowerets)	2 to 2½ min	**3½ to 4 min**
Corn, whole kernel	1¼ to 1½ min	**2 to 2½ min**
Corn on the cob	4 to 5 min (1 ear)	**6 to 8 min (2 ears)**
Mixed vegetables	1¼ to 1½ min	**2½ to 3 min**
Onions, small whole	1½ to 2 min	**2½ to 3 min**
Peas, green	1 to 1½ min	**2½ to 3 min**
Potatoes, white or sweet	conventional cooking recommended	

Canned Vegetables: Drain 8- to 9-oz can of vegetables, reserving 1 tbsp liquid for each ½ cup serving. Mix vegetables and liquid in casserole. Cover tightly and microwave on high (550 watts) 30 sec to 1½ min [**1 to 2½ min**].

Asparagus Parmesan

1 Serving	[2 Servings]
⅔ cup frozen cut asparagus	1⅓ cups frozen cut asparagus
1 tsp margarine or butter	2 tsp margarine or butter
3 mushrooms, thinly sliced	6 mushrooms, thinly sliced
Dash of garlic powder	⅛ tsp garlic powder
Freshly ground pepper	Freshly ground pepper
2 tsp grated Parmesan cheese	1 tbsp plus 1 tsp grated Parmesan cheese

Place asparagus and margarine in 12-oz casserole [24-oz casserole]. Cover with vented plastic wrap and microwave on high (550 watts) 2 min [4 min]. Stir in mushrooms, garlic powder and pepper. Cover with vented plastic wrap and microwave until tender, 45 sec to 1½ min [2 to 3 min]. Stir in Parmesan cheese.

Saucy Asparagus

1 Serving	[2 Servings]
3 tbsp shredded process sharp American cheese	⅓ cup shredded process sharp American cheee
1 tsp milk	2 tsp milk
Dash of dry mustard	⅛ tsp dry mustard
½ can (8-oz size) cut asparagus spears, drained	1 can (8 oz) cut asparagus spears, drained
1 round buttery cracker, crushed	2 round buttery crackers, crushed

Place cheese, milk and mustard in 1-cup measure. Microwave uncovered on medium (275 watts) 30 sec [45 sec]; stir. Microwave uncovered until cheese is melted, about 15 sec longer [about 45 sec longer].

Place asparagus in 8-oz casserole [15-oz casserole]. Cover with vented plastic wrap and microwave on high (550 watts) until hot, 45 to 60 sec [1½ to 2 min]. Pour cheese mixture over top; sprinkle with cracker crumbs.

Green Beans with Cream

1 Serving	[2 Servings]
1 tsp water	2 tsp water
⅛ tsp onion salt	¼ tsp onion salt
Dash of pepper	⅛ tsp pepper
Dash of dried basil leaves	Dash of dried basil leaves
⅔ cup frozen cut green beans	1⅓ cups frozen cut green beans
1 tsp margarine or butter	2 tsp margarine or butter
1 tbsp whipping cream or half-and-half	2 tbsp whipping cream or half-and-half

Place water, onion salt, pepper, basil and beans in 12-oz casserole [24-oz casserole]; dot with margarine. Cover with vented plastic wrap and microwave on high (550 watts) until tender, 3 to 4 min [4 to 6 min, stirring after 3 min]. Stir in cream. Cover and microwave until cream is hot, about 30 sec [about 1 min].

Dilled Green Beans

1 Serving	[2 Servings]
⅔ cup frozen cut green beans	1⅓ cups frozen cut green beans
1 tsp margarine or butter	2 tsp margarine or butter
1 tsp vinegar	2 tsp vinegar
Dash of garlic salt	⅛ tsp garlic salt
Dash of dried dill weed	⅛ tsp dried dill weed
Dash of pepper	⅛ tsp pepper

Mix all ingredients in 12-oz casserole [24-oz casserole]. Cover with vented plastic wrap and microwave on high (550 watts) 2 min; stir. Cover with vented plastic wrap and microwave until tender, 1½ to 2½ min [3 to 5 min].

Sliced Beets with Oranges

Sliced Beets with Oranges

1 Serving	[2 Servings]
½ can (8¼-oz size) sliced beets, drained	1 can (8¼ oz) sliced beets, drained
½ orange, pared and cut into ¼" slices	1 orange, pared and cut into ¼" slices
1 tsp margarine or butter	2 tsp margarine or butter
Dash of salt	Dash of salt
Dash of pepper	Dash of pepper

Alternate beets (2 or 3 slices at a time) and orange slices in 12-oz shallow casserole [24-oz shallow casserole]. Dot with margarine. Cover with vented plastic wrap and microwave on high (550 watts) until hot, 1 to 2 min [2 to 3 min]. Sprinkle with salt and pepper.

Savory Broccoli

1 Serving	[2 Servings]
2 spears broccoli (1 oz)	4 spears broccoli (2 oz)
2 tsp water	1 tbsp water
1½ tsp margarine or butter	1 tbsp margarine or butter
¼ tsp prepared horseradish	½ tsp prepared horseradish
Dash of salt	⅛ tsp salt
Dash of dry mustard	⅛ tsp dry mustard

Cut broccoli lengthwise into thin spears. Arrange broccoli in 22-oz casserole [9 × 1¼" pie plate] with tips in center; add water. Cover tightly and microwave on high (550 watts) 1 min; rotate casserole [pie plate] ½ turn. Microwave until tender, 1½ to 2 min longer [4 to 4½ min longer]. Let stand covered 1 min; drain.

Place remaining ingredients in 6-oz custard cup. Cover with vented plastic wrap and microwave on high (550 watts) until margarine is melted, about 15 sec [about 30 sec]; stir. Pour over broccoli. Sprinkle with paprika if desired.

89

Broccoli with Swiss Cheese

1 Serving	[2 Servings]
1 tsp water	2 tsp water
1/8 tsp instant minced onion	1/4 tsp instant minced onion
Dash of salt	1/8 tsp salt
Dash of pepper	1/8 tsp pepper
2/3 cup frozen cut broccoli	1 1/3 cups frozen cut broccoli
1 tsp margarine or butter	2 tsp margarine or butter
2 tbsp shredded Swiss cheese	1/4 cup shredded Swiss cheese

Mix water, onion, salt, pepper and broccoli in 12-oz casserole [24-oz casserole]. Dot with margarine. Cover with vented plastic wrap and microwave on high (550 watts) until crisp-tender, 2 to 3 min [3 to 4 min]; stir. Sprinkle with cheese.

Creamy Cabbage

1 Serving	[2 Servings]
1 tbsp water	2 tbsp water
1/4 tsp celery salt	1/2 tsp celery salt
Dash of garlic powder	Dash of garlic powder
1 1/2 cups finely shredded cabbage	3 cups finely shredded cabbage
2 tbsp whipped cream cheese	1/4 cup whipped cream cheese
2 tsp milk	1 tbsp plus 1 tsp milk
1/8 tsp celery seed	1/4 tsp celery seed
Freshly ground pepper	Freshly ground pepper

Mix water, celery salt, garlic powder and cabbage in 15-oz casserole [1-qt casserole]. Cover with vented plastic wrap and microwave on high (550 watts) until crisp-tender, 2 to 3 min [3 to 4 min]. Mix remaining ingredients; stir into hot cabbage.

Brussels Sprouts and Tomatoes

1 Serving	[2 Servings]
2 tsp water	1 tbsp water
Dash of salt	1/8 tsp salt
Freshly ground pepper	Freshly ground pepper
1/2 cup frozen baby Brussels sprouts	1 cup frozen baby Brussels sprouts
1 tsp margarine or butter	2 tsp margarine or butter
3 cherry tomatoes, cut into halves	6 cherry tomatoes, cut into halves

Mix water, salt, pepper and Brussels sprouts in 12-oz casserole [24-oz casserole]. Dot with margarine. Cover with vented plastic wrap and microwave on high (550 watts) until tender, 2 to 3 min [4 to 5 min]. Stir in tomatoes. Cover with vented plastic wrap and microwave until tomatoes are hot, 30 to 40 sec [40 to 50 sec].

Gingered Chinese Cabbage

1 Serving	[2 Servings]
1 tsp vegetable oil	2 tsp vegetable oil
1/4 tsp grated gingerroot	1/2 tsp grated gingerroot
1 1/2 tsp water	1 tbsp water
1 1/2 tsp soy sauce	1 tbsp soy sauce
Dash of sugar	Dash of sugar
1 1/2 cups finely shredded Chinese cabbage	3 cups finely shredded Chinese cabbage

Mix all ingredients in 12-oz casserole [1-qt casserole]. Cover with vented plastic wrap and microwave on high (550 watts) until crisp-tender, 2 to 2 1/2 min [3 to 3 1/2 min]; stir. Sprinkle with finely chopped fully cooked smoked ham if desired.

Brussels Sprouts and Tomatoes, Potato with Toppers (page 98), Buttery Fish Fillet (page 41)

Shredded Carrots, One Rib Roast (page 13)

Shredded Carrots

1 Serving	[**2 Servings**]
1 slice bacon, cut into ½" pieces	***2 slices bacon, cut into ½" pieces***
¾ cup coarsely shredded carrot (1 large)	***1½ cups coarsely shredded carrots (2 large)***
1 finely chopped green onion (with top)	***2 finely chopped green onions (with tops)***
1 tsp lemon juice	***2 tsp lemon juice***
Dash of salt	***Dash of salt***
Dash of pepper	***Dash of pepper***

Place bacon in 2-cup measure [**4-cup measure**]. Cover loosely and microwave on high (550 watts) until crisp, 2 to 2½ min [**3 to 3½ min**]. Remove bacon with slotted spoon; crumble and reserve.

Stir remaining ingredients into fat. Cover with vented plastic wrap and microwave until crisp-tender, 2½ to 3 min [**3½ to 4 min**]. Sprinkle with bacon.

Glazed Carrots

1 Serving	[**2 Servings**]
1 tbsp packed brown sugar	***2 tbsp packed brown sugar***
½ tsp cornstarch	***1 tsp cornstarch***
Dash of ground cinnamon	***⅛ tsp ground cinnamon***
3 tbsp orange juice	***⅓ cup orange juice***
¾ cup ¼" slices carrots	***1½ cups ¼" slices carrots***
1½ tsp margarine or butter	***1 tbsp margarine or butter***

Place carrots in 12-oz casserole [**24-oz casserole**]. Mix brown sugar, cornstarch and cinnamon in 12-oz casserole [**24-oz casserole**]; stir in orange juice. Stir in carrots; dot with margarine. Cover with vented plastic wrap and microwave on high (550 watts) 3 min [**4 min**]; stir. Cover with vented plastic wrap and microwave until crisp-tender, 1 to 3 min longer [**2 to 4 min longer**].

Zippy Carrots, Sole on Deviled Stuffing (page 43), Cauliflower Italian, Wine Poached Salmon (page 44)

Zippy Carrots

1 Serving	**[2 Servings]**
½ tsp instant beef bouillon	**1 tsp instant beef bouillon**
⅛ tsp dry mustard	**¼ tsp dry mustard**
⅛ tsp salt	**¼ tsp salt**
2 tbsp hot water	**¼ cup hot water**
3 drops red pepper sauce	**6 drops red pepper sauce**
¾ cup ⅜" strips carrots (2" long)	**1½ cups ⅜" strips carrots (2" long)**
1 tsp margarine or butter	**2 tsp margarine or butter**

Mix bouillon (dry), mustard, salt, water and pepper sauce in 12-oz casserole [**1-qt casserole**]. Stir in carrots; dot with margarine. Cover with vented plastic wrap and microwave on high (550 watts) until tender, 3 to 4 min [**5 to 7 min**]; stir. Sprinkle with snipped parsley if desired.

Cauliflower Italian

1 Serving	**[2 Servings]**
½ cup frozen small cauliflowerets	**1 cup frozen small cauliflowerets**
¼ medium green pepper, cut into ¼" strips	**½ medium green pepper, cut into ¼" strips**
1½ tsp olive oil or vegetable oil	**1 tbsp olive oil or vegetable oil**
⅛ tsp dried oregano leaves	**¼ tsp dried oregano leaves**
⅛ tsp salt	**¼ tsp salt**
Dash of garlic powder	**⅛ tsp garlic powder**

Place cauliflower and green pepper in 12-oz casserole [**24-oz casserole**]. Mix remaining ingredients; drizzle over vegetables. Cover with vented plastic wrap and microwave on high (550 watts) until vegetables are crisp-tender, 2 to 3 min [**3 to 4 min**]; stir. Sprinkle with grated Parmesan cheese if desired.

Cauliflower and Peas

1 Serving	[2 Servings]
2 tsp water	1 tbsp plus 1 tsp water
Dash of salt	1/8 tsp salt
Freshly ground pepper	Freshly ground pepper
1/2 cup frozen small cauliflowerets	1 cup frozen small cauliflowerets
1/4 cup frozen green peas	1/2 cup frozen green peas
1 1/2 tsp margarine or butter	1 tbsp margarine or butter
1 tbsp blue cheese dressing	2 tbsp blue cheese dressing

Place water, salt, pepper, cauliflower and peas in 12-oz casserole [**24-oz casserole**]. Dot with margarine. Cover with vented plastic wrap and microwave on high (550 watts) until vegetables are crisp-tender, 3 to 4 min [**4 to 5 min**]; stir. Drizzle with blue cheese dressing.

Peppery Corn and Tomatoes

1 Serving	[2 Servings]
1 tsp water	2 tsp water
1/8 tsp garlic powder	1/4 tsp garlic powder
1/8 tsp salt	1/4 tsp salt
Dash of ground red pepper	Dash of ground red pepper
2/3 cup frozen whole kernel corn	1 1/3 cups frozen whole kernel corn
1 green onion (with top), chopped	2 green onions (with tops), chopped
1 tsp margarine or butter	2 tsp margarine or butter
1/4 medium tomato, chopped	1/2 medium tomato, chopped

Place water, garlic powder, salt, red pepper, corn and onion in 12-oz casserole [**24-oz casserole**]. Cover with vented plastic wrap and microwave on high (550 watts) until corn is tender, 2 1/2 to 3 1/2 min [**4 to 5 min**]. Stir in margarine and tomato. Cover with vented plastic wrap and microwave until tomato is hot, about 30 sec. [**about 1 min**].

Country-style Limas

1 Serving	[2 Servings]
1 slice bacon, cut into 1/2" pieces	2 slices bacon, cut into 1/2" pieces
2/3 cup frozen baby lima beans	1 1/3 cups frozen baby lima beans
1 tbsp finely chopped onion	2 tbsp finely chopped onion
2 tbsp tomato juice	1/4 cup tomato juice
1 tsp molasses	2 tsp molasses
1 tsp chili sauce	2 tsp chili sauce
1/2 tsp packed brown sugar	1 tsp packed brown sugar
1/4 tsp prepared mustard	1/2 tsp prepared mustard

Place bacon in 12-oz casserole [**24-oz casserole**]. Cover loosely and microwave on high (550 watts) until almost crisp, 1 to 2 min [**2 to 3 min**]. Remove bacon with slotted spoon; crumble and reserve.

Stir remaining ingredients into bacon fat. Cover with vented plastic wrap and microwave 2 min [**4 min**]; stir. Cover with vented plastic wrap and microwave until beans are tender, 1 1/2 to 2 1/2 min longer [**1 1/2 to 4 min longer**]. Sprinkle with bacon.

Corn with Cream

1 Serving	[2 Servings]
2/3 cup frozen whole kernel corn	1 1/3 cups frozen whole kernel corn
1 tsp margarine or butter	2 tsp margarine or butter
Dash of salt	1/8 tsp salt
Dash of pepper	1/8 tsp pepper
Dash of ground nutmeg	1/8 tsp ground nutmeg
2 tbsp whipping cream or half-and-half	1/4 cup whipping cream or half-and-half

Place all ingredients except cream in 12-oz casserole [**24-oz casserole**]. Cover with vented plastic wrap and microwave on high (550 watts) until tender, 1 1/2 to 2 1/2 min [**3 to 4 min**]. Stir in cream. Cover with vented plastic wrap and microwave until hot, 20 to 30 sec [**30 to 40 sec**].

Rosy Onions

1 Serving	[2 Servings]
1½ tsp margarine or butter	1 tbsp margarine or butter
1 tsp all-purpose flour	2 tsp all-purpose flour
¼ tsp instant beef bouillon	½ tsp instant beef bouillon
2 tbsp water	¼ cup water
1 tbsp catsup	2 tbsp catsup
1 tbsp dry red wine	2 tbsp dry red wine
Dash of dried thyme leaves	Dash of dried thyme leaves
Dash of salt	⅛ tsp salt
⅔ cup frozen small whole onions	1⅓ cups frozen small whole onions

Place margarine in 12-oz casserole [24-oz casserole]. Microwave uncovered on high (550 watts) until melted, 15 to 25 sec [30 to 45 sec]. Mix in flour and bouillon (dry). Stir in water, catsup, wine, thyme and salt; add onions. Cover with vented plastic wrap and microwave until onions are hot and tender, 3 to 4 min [5 to 7 min]; stir.

Mushrooms in Wine

1 Serving	[2 Servings]
1 tsp margarine or butter	2 tsp margarine or butter
½ tsp cornstarch	1 tsp cornstarch
Dash of salt	⅛ tsp salt
1 tbsp dry white wine	2 tbsp dry white wine
4 oz mushrooms, cut into halves (1½ cups)	8 oz mushrooms, cut into halves (3 cups)
½ small clove garlic, finely chopped	1 small clove garlic, finely chopped
Snipped parsley	Snipped parsley

Place all ingredients except parsley in 15-oz casserole [1-qt casserole]. Cover loosely and microwave on high (550 watts) 1 min [2 min]; stir. Cover loosely and microwave until hot, 30 to 60 sec longer [1 to 1½ min longer]. Sprinkle with parsley.

Rosy Onions

Peas with Mushrooms and Tomatoes, Potato with Toppers (page 98), Chicken Pieces (page 51)

Peas with Mushrooms and Tomatoes

1 Serving	[2 Servings]
1 tsp water	2 tsp water
1/8 tsp salt	1/4 tsp salt
Dash of pepper	Dash of pepper
1/2 cup frozen green peas	1 cup frozen green peas
1 tsp margarine or butter	2 tsp margarine or butter
2 mushrooms, thinly sliced	4 mushrooms, thinly sliced
2 cherry tomatoes, cut into halves	4 cherry tomatoes, cut into halves

Place water, salt and pepper in 12-oz casserole [**24-oz casserole**]. Stir in peas; dot with margarine. Cover with vented plastic wrap and microwave on high (550 watts) until tender, 2½ to 3½ min [**3½ to 4½ min**]. Stir in mushrooms and tomatoes. Cover with vented plastic wrap and microwave until tomatoes are hot, 30 to 60 sec [**45 sec to 1½ min**].

Garlicky Green Onions

1 Serving	[2 Servings]
1½ tsp margarine or butter	1 tbsp margarine or butter
1/4 tsp garlic powder	1/2 tsp garlic powder
1/8 tsp ground ginger	1/4 tsp ground ginger
Dash of salt	1/8 tsp salt
Freshly ground pepper	Freshly ground pepper
6 green onions (with tops), cut into 5" pieces	12 green onions (with tops), cut into 5" pieces

Place all ingredients except onion in 12-oz shallow casserole [**24-oz shallow casserole**]. Microwave uncovered on high (550 watts) until margarine is melted, 15 to 25 sec [**25 to 35 sec**]; stir. Place onions in margarine mixture; roll to coat. Cover with vented plastic wrap and microwave until crisp-tender, 30 to 60 sec [**45 to 60 sec**].

Peas and Cucumber

1 Serving	[2 Servings]
1 tsp water	2 tsp water
Dash of salt	1/8 tsp salt
Dash of pepper	1/8 tsp pepper
Dash of dried dill weed	1/8 tsp dried dill weed
1/2 cup frozen green peas	1 cup frozen green peas
1 tsp margarine or butter	2 tsp margarine or butter
1/4 cup diced cucumber	1/2 cup diced cucumber

Mix water, salt, pepper and dill weed in 12-oz casserole [24-oz casserole]. Stir in peas; dot with margarine. Cover with vented plastic wrap and microwave on high (550 watts) until tender, 2½ to 3½ min [5 to 6 min]. Stir in cucumber. Cover with vented plastic wrap and microwave until cucumber is hot, about 30 sec [about 1 min]. Sprinkle with grated Parmesan cheese if desired.

Potato with Toppers

1 Serving	[2 Servings]
1 medium baking potato Toppers (below)	2 medium baking potatoes Toppers (below)

Prick potato[es] with fork to allow steam to escape. Microwave uncovered 3 min; turn potato[es] over. Microwave uncovered until tender, 1½ to 2 min [3½ to 5 min]. Wrap potato[es] in aluminum foil; let stand 5 min. Split top[s] of potato[es] and squeeze gently until some potato pops up through opening; top with one of the Toppers.

Toppers

Dairy sour cream and finely chopped green onion (with top)

Hot cooked chopped broccoli and shredded mozzarela cheese

Diced fully cooked smoked ham and chili sauce

Crisply cooked bacon pieces and shredded process American cheese

Chopped shrimp and whipped cream cheese

Peppers and Mushrooms

1 Serving	[2 Servings]
1½ tsp margarine	1 tbsp margarine
1/8 tsp red pepper sauce	1/4 tsp red pepper sauce
Dash of salt	1/8 tsp salt
1/2 medium green pepper, cut into 1/4" strips	1 medium green pepper, cut into 1/4" strips
1/8" slice medium onion, separated into rings	Two 1/8" slices medium onion, separated into rings
3 mushrooms, thinly sliced	6 mushrooms, thinly sliced

Place margarine in 12-oz shallow casserole [24-oz shallow casserole]. Microwave uncovered on high (550 watts) until melted, 15 to 25 sec [30 to 45 sec]. Mix in pepper sauce and salt. Stir in remaining ingredients. Cover with vented plastic wrap and microwave until green pepper is crisp-tender, 2 to 3 min [3 to 4 min]. Serve over grilled steak if desired.

Peppers and Mushrooms

Stuffed Potato

1 Serving	[2 Servings]
1 large baking potato	2 large baking potatoes
2 tbsp milk	1/4 cup milk
2 tbsp dairy sour cream	1/4 cup dairy sour cream
1 tbsp margarine	2 tbsp margarine
2 tbsp snipped dried beef	1/4 cup snipped dried beef
1 tbsp finely chopped green onion (with top)	2 tbsp finely chopped green onion (with top)
Dash of salt	1/8 tsp salt
Dash of pepper	1/8 tsp pepper
2 tbsp shredded process American cheese	1/4 cup shredded process American cheese

Prick potato[es] with fork to allow steam to escape. Microwave uncovered on high (550 watts) 3 min; turn potato[es] over. Microwave uncovered until tender, 2 to 4 min [4 to 6 min]. Wrap potato[es] in aluminum foil; let stand 5 min.

Cut thin lengthwise slice from top[s] of potato[es]; scoop out inside[s], leaving thin shell[s]. Mash potato, milk, sour cream and margarine. Stir in beef, onion, salt and pepper. Fill shell[s] with potato mixture. Cover with waxed paper and microwave on medium (275 watts) until hot, 2 to 3 min [4 to 5 min]. Sprinkle with cheese. Microwave uncovered on high (550 watts) until cheese is melted, about 30 sec [about 1 min].

Sweet Potato

1 Serving	[2 Servings]
1 medium sweet potato	2 medium sweet potatoes
1 tbsp margarine	2 tbsp margarine
1 tbsp maple-flavored syrup	2 tbsp maple-flavored syrup
1 tbsp chopped pecans	2 tbsp chopped pecans

Prick potato[es] with fork to allow steam to escape. Microwave uncovered on high (550 watts) 3 min; turn potato[es] over. Microwave uncovered until tender, 1½ to 2 min [2½ to 4 min]. Wrap in aluminum foil; let stand 5 min.

Slit top[s] of potato[es] and squeeze until some potato pops up through opening; top with margarine. Drizzle with syrup and sprinkle with pecans.

Stuffed Potato, Sweet Potato

Corn-filled Tomato

1 Serving	[2 Servings]
1 large tomato	2 large tomatoes
1 slice bacon, cut into ½" pieces	2 slices bacon, cut into ½" pieces
½ can (7-oz size) whole kernel corn, drained	1 can (7 oz) whole kernel corn, drained
2 tsp finely chopped green onion (with top)	1 tbsp plus 1 tsp finely chopped green onion (with top)
Freshly ground pepper	Freshly ground pepper

Remove stem from tomato[es]. Scoop out pulp, leaving ½" wall[s]. Chop pulp; reserve. Place bacon in 2-cup measure [4-cup measure]. Cover loosely and microwave on high (550 watts) until almost crisp, 1¼ to 2½ min [2½ to 4 min]; drain.

Mix bacon, tomato pulp and remaining ingredients. Fill tomato[es] with corn mixture; place in 10-oz casserole [two 10-oz casseroles]. Spoon remaining corn mixture around tomato[es]. Cover with waxed paper and microwave on high (550 watts) until tomato is hot, 1¼ to 2 min [2½ to 4 min].

Garlic Tomato Sauce

1 Serving	[2 Servings]
Prepare Garlic Tomato Sauce for 2 Servings. Cover and refrigerate any remaining sauce. To reheat, cover with waxed paper and microwave on high (550 watts) until hot.	1½ tsp olive oil or vegetable oil
	2 cloves garlic, finely chopped
	1 can (8 oz) stewed tomatoes
	½ can (6-oz size) tomato paste
	⅛ tsp salt
	⅛ tsp dried basil leaves
	⅛ tsp dried oregano leaves
	Dash of sugar
	Freshly ground pepper

Place olive oil and garlic in 24-oz casserole. Cover with waxed paper and microwave on high (550 watts) until garlic is tender, 1 to 2 min. Stir in remaining ingredients. Cover and microwave 2 min; stir. Cover and microwave until hot and bubbly, 2 to 3 min longer. Serve over hot pasta and sprinkle with Parmesan cheese if desired.

Corn-filled Tomato, Salisbury-style Steak (page 18)

Layered Zucchini and Tomato

Layered Zucchini and Tomato

1 Serving	[2 Servings]
½ cup ¼" slices zucchini	1 cup ¼" slices zucchini
1 tbsp sliced green onion (with top)	2 tbsp sliced green onion (with top)
Dash of salt	⅛ tsp salt
Dash of dried basil leaves	⅛ tsp dried basil leaves
Dash of pepper	Dash of pepper
½ medium tomato, cut into ½" slices	1 medium tomato, cut into ½" slices
2 tbsp dairy sour cream	¼ cup dairy sour cream
1 tsp grated Parmesan cheese	2 tsp grated Parmesan cheese

Mix zucchini, onion, salt, basil and pepper in 16-oz casserole [**1-qt casserole**]. Cover with waxed paper and microwave on high (550 watts) until zucchini is crisp-tender, 30 to 60 sec [**1 to 1½ min**]; stir. Place tomato slices on zucchini. Mix sour cream and cheese; spread over tomato slices. Cover with waxed paper and microwave on medium-low (165 watts) until tomato slices are warm, 1 to 2 min [**1½ to 2 min**]. Sprinkle with additional Parmesan cheese if desired.

Zucchini and Carrots Basil

1 Serving	[2 Servings]
½ cup ¼" slices zucchini	1 cup ¼" slices zucchini
2 tbsp shredded carrot	¼ cup shredded carrot
1½ tsp margarine or butter	1 tbsp margarine or butter
½ tsp snipped basil	1 tsp snipped basil
Dash of salt	Dash of salt
Freshly ground pepper	Freshly ground pepper

Mix all ingredients except pepper in 13-oz casserole [**16-oz casserole**]. Cover tightly and microwave on high (550 watts) 30 to 60 sec [**1 to 1½ min**]; stir. Cover tightly and microwave until crisp-tender, about 30 sec longer [**30 to 60 sec longer**]. Sprinkle with pepper.

Squash with Sausage Stuffing

1 Serving	[2 Servings]
1 acorn squash half (½ lb)	2 acorn squash halves (1 lb)
½ cup herb-seasoned stuffing mix	1 cup herb-seasoned stuffing mix
¼ cup chopped fully cooked Polish sausage	½ cup chopped fully cooked Polish sausage
2 tbsp margarine or butter, melted	¼ cup margarine or butter, melted
1 tbsp hot water	2 tbsp hot water
Dash of pepper	⅛ tsp pepper

Remove seeds from squash. Place squash, cut side[s] down, in 8 × 8 × 2" dish. Cover tightly and microwave on high (550 watts) until tender, 3 to 4 min [**6 to 7 min**]. Cut thin slice from pointed end[s]. Arrange squash, cut side[s] up, in dish.

Mix remaining ingredients. Spoon into squash. Cover tightly and microwave until stuffing is hot, 1½ to 2 min [**1½ to 2 min**].

Buttercup Squash with Apples

1 Serving	[2 Servings]
¼ small buttercup squash (¼ lb)	½ small buttercup squash (½ lb)
¼ cup chopped tart apple	½ cup chopped tart apple
1 tsp packed brown sugar	2 tsp packed brown sugar
1 tsp margarine or butter, softened	2 tsp margarine or butter, softened
¼ tsp lemon juice	½ tsp lemon juice
Dash of ground nutmeg	Dash of ground nutmeg

Cut squash into fourths; remove seeds and fibers. Place squash, cut sides up, in 9 × 1¼" pie plate. Mix remaining ingredients; spoon into squash. Cover with waxed paper and microwave on high (550 watts) 1 min [**2 min**]; rotate plate ½ turn. Microwave until tender, 1½ to 2½ min [**2 to 3 min**]. Spoon juices over squash.

Squash with Sausage Stuffing, Buttercup Squash with Apples

Herbed Biscuit Ring

1 Serving	**[2 Servings]**
Prepare Herbed Biscuit Ring for 2 servings. Reheat half of the ring for another meal. See Bread Reheat Chart, page 107.	**2 tbsp margarine or butter** **1 cup buttermilk baking mix** **⅓ cup milk** **Herb-Cheese Coating (below)**

Place margarine in 10-oz custard cup. Microwave uncovered on high (550 watts) until melted, 30 to 40 sec; reserve. Mix baking mix and milk until soft dough forms; beat vigorously 15 sec. Turn onto surface well floured with baking mix; turn to coat. Knead 10 times. Divide dough into 6 equal parts; shape into balls. Dip into margarine to coat completely. Roll in Herb-Cheese Coating.

Place 6-oz juice glass in center of 1-qt casserole. Place balls in casserole. Place casserole on inverted plate in microwave oven. Microwave uncovered on medium (275 watts) 2 min; rotate casserole ½ turn. Microwave uncovered until no longer doughy, 2 to 2½ min longer. Remove glass. Invert ring on serving plate.

Herb-Cheese Coating

Mix ¼ cup grated Parmesan cheese, ½ tsp dried Italian seasoning and ¼ tsp paprika.

Boston Brown Bread

1 Serving	**[2 Servings]**
Prepare Brown Bread for 2 Servings. Reheat half of the loaf for another meal. See Bread Reheat Chart, page 107.	**½ cup buttermilk** **¼ cup all-purpose flour** **¼ cup whole wheat flour (not stone-ground)** **¼ cup cornmeal** **3 tbsp molasses** **½ tsp baking soda** **¼ tsp salt** **⅓ cup raisins**

Beat all ingredients except raisins in 1-qt bowl on low speed, scraping bowl constantly, 30 sec. Beat on medium speed, scraping bowl constantly, 30 sec. Stir in raisins. Pour into greased 2-cup measure. Cover tightly and microwave on medium (275 watts) 3 min; rotate measure ¼ turn. Microwave until no longer doughy, 2 to 3 min longer. Let stand uncovered 5 min; remove from measure. Serve warm with softened margarine, butter or cream cheese if desired.

Apple-Streusel Muffins

1 Serving	[2 Servings]
Prepare Apple-Streusel Muffins for 2 Servings. Reheat half of the muffins for another meal. See Bread Reheat Chart, page 107.	¾ **cup buttermilk baking mix**
	2 **tbsp sugar**
	3 **tbsp sweetened applesauce**
	1 **tbsp vegetable oil**
	½ **tsp vanilla**
	1 **egg**
	Streusel Topping (below)

Line 6 medium muffin cups, 2½ × 1¼", with paper baking cups. Or arrange six 6-oz custard cups in circle on 12" plate; line with paper baking cups. Mix all ingredients except Streusel Topping until moistened. Fill muffin cups ⅔ full. Sprinkle with Streusel Topping. Microwave uncovered on high (550 watts) 1 min; rotate plate ½ turn. Microwave uncovered until tops spring back when touched lightly and are almost dry, 1½ to 2 min longer. Let stand uncovered 1 min; remove from cups.

Streusel Topping

Mix 2 tbsp buttermilk baking mix, 2 tbsp packed brown sugar, 1 tbsp finely chopped nuts, 1 tsp firm margarine or butter and ¼ tsp ground cinnamon until crumbly.

Savory Bun Halves

1 Serving	[2 Servings]
1 *frankfurter or hamburger bun, split* One of the seasoned spreads (below)	2 **frankfurters or hamburger buns, split** **One of the seasoned spreads (below)**

Spread cut sides of bun[s] with one of the seasoned spreads. Place on plate. Cover with waxed paper and microwave on medium (275 watts) until bread is warm, 35 to 45 sec [**1 to 1¼ min**]. Cut into halves if desired.

Chili-Cheese Spread: Mix 2 tbsp [**¼ cup**] shredded sharp Cheddar cheese, 1 tbsp [**2 tbsp**] margarine or butter, softened, 1 tsp [**2 tsp**] chopped green chilies and dash [**dash**] of Worcestershire sauce.

Herb-Cheese Spread: Mix 1 tbsp [**2 tbsp**] margarine or butter, softened, 1 tsp [**2 tsp**] grated Parmesan cheese, ½ tsp [**1 tsp**] Italian seasoning and dash [**dash**] of garlic powder.

Onion Spread: Mix 1 tbsp [**2 tbsp**] margarine or butter, softened, and 1½ tsp [**1 tbsp**] chopped green onion (with top).

Dill and Garlic Croutons

1 Serving	[2 Servings]
2 *tsp margarine or butter*	1 **tbsp margarine or butter**
⅛ *tsp dried dill weed*	¼ **tsp dried dill weed**
⅛ *tsp paprika*	¼ **tsp paprika**
Dash of garlic salt	⅛ **tsp garlic salt**
½ *cup ½" bread cubes*	1 **cup ½" bread cubes**

Place margarine in 10-oz casserole [**22-oz casserole**]. Microwave uncovered on high (550 watts) until melted, 35 to 45 sec [**45 to 60 sec**]. Stir in dill weed, paprika and garlic salt. Add bread cubes; toss until coated. Microwave uncovered until crisp and dry, 1½ to 2 min [**2 to 2½ min**].

Caramel-Pecan Coffee Cake

1 Serving	[**2 Servings**]

Prepare Caramel-Pecan Coffee Cake for 2 Servings. Reheat half of the coffee cake for another meal. See Bread Reheat Chart, page 107.

2 tbsp margarine or butter
¼ cup packed brown sugar
2 tbsp chopped pecans
2 tbsp light corn syrup
¼ tsp ground cinnamon
1 cup buttermilk baking mix
¼ cup cold water

Place margarine in 1-qt casserole. Microwave uncovered on high (550 watts) until melted, 20 to 30 sec. Stir in brown sugar, pecans, corn syrup and cinnamon; spread evenly in casserole. Microwave uncovered until bubbly, 45 to 60 sec. Tilt casserole so brown sugar mixture runs to side; place 6-oz juice glass in center of casserole.

Mix baking mix and water until soft dough forms. Drop dough by 6 spoonfuls onto brown sugar mixture. Place casserole on inverted plate in microwave oven. Microwave uncovered on medium-high (385 watts) 2 min; rotate casserole ½ turn. Microwave uncovered until wooden pick inserted in center comes out clean, 2 to 2½ min longer. Remove glass. Immediately invert on heatproof serving plate; let casserole remain 1 min so caramel can drizzle over coffee cake. Serve warm.

Cheesy French Slices

1 Serving	[2 Servings]
1 individual French roll	2 individual French rolls
1½ tsp margarine or butter	1 tbsp margarine or butter
1½ tsp crumbled blue cheese	1 tbsp crumbled blue cheese
½ tsp grated Parmesan cheese	1 tsp grated Parmesan cheese

Cut roll[s] diagonally into 1" slices. Place margarine and blue cheese in 6-oz custard cup. Microwave uncovered on medium-low (165 watts) until softened, 15 to 20 sec [20 to 30 sec]. Stir in Parmesan cheese; spread over 1 side of each slice bread. Reassemble roll[s]; place on plate. Cover with waxed paper and microwave on medium (275 watts) until warm, 30 to 40 sec [1 to 1½ min].

Hot Cooked Rice

1 Serving	[2 Servings]
⅔ cup uncooked instant rice	1⅓ cups uncooked instant rice
⅔ cup water	1⅓ cups water
¼ tsp salt	½ tsp salt

Mix all ingredients in 22-oz casserole [1-qt casserole]. Cover tightly and microwave on high (550 watts) until rice is tender and water is absorbed, 3 to 4 min [6 to 7 min]; stir.

Spanish Rice

1 Serving	[2 Servings]
2 slices bacon, cut into ½" pieces	4 slices bacon, cut into ½" pieces
½ cup uncooked instant rice	1 cup uncooked instant rice
⅓ cup hot water	⅔ cup hot water
¼ cup coarsely chopped tomato	½ cup coarsely chopped tomato
2 tbsp chopped green pepper	¼ cup chopped green pepper
2 tbsp chopped onion	¼ cup chopped onion
¼ tsp salt	½ tsp salt
¼ tsp chili powder	½ tsp chili powder
Dash of pepper	⅛ tsp pepper

Place bacon in 22-oz casserole [1-qt casserole]. Cover loosely and microwave on high (550 watts) until almost crisp, 2½ to 3 min [4½ to 6 min]. Stir in remaining ingredients. Cover tightly and microwave 1 min [2 min]; stir. Cover tightly and microwave until rice is tender and water is absorbed, 1 to 2 min longer [1 to 2 min longer].

Cheesy Rice Casserole

1 Serving	[2 Servings]
¼ cup dairy sour cream	½ cup dairy sour cream
2 tbsp finely chopped green pepper	¼ cup finely chopped green pepper
¼ tsp dry mustard	½ tsp dry mustard
⅛ tsp salt	¼ tsp salt
3 drops red pepper sauce	6 drops red pepper sauce
¾ cup hot cooked rice	1½ cups hot cooked rice
¼ cup shredded mozzarella cheese	½ cup shredded mozzarella cheese
1 tsp grated Parmesan cheese	2 tsp grated Parmesan cheese
1 tsp snipped parsley	2 tsp snipped parsley

Mix sour cream, green pepper, mustard, salt and pepper sauce. Layer ¼ cup [½ cup] of the rice and ½ each of the sour cream mixture and mozzarella cheese in 10-oz casserole [22-oz casserole]; repeat. Spread top with remaining rice. Cover with vented plastic wrap and microwave on medium-high (385 watts) until hot, 3 to 4 min [4 to 5 min]. Sprinkle with Parmesan cheese and parsley.

Reheating Breads

Biscuits, muffins, bagels, croissants, coffee cake, rolls and special breads are best served warm. To reheat, place the amount you need on a microwavable plate, cover with waxed paper and microwave as directed below. To avoid overheating, use medium power level setting (275 watts). Because breads are porous and cook quickly, always check for doneness at minimum time. Breads should be warm, not hot and steamy. Overheating toughens breads and causes fillings, frostings and fruits in breads to get too hot because they heat even more quickly than breads do.

Bread	Amount 1 Serving	[2 Servings]	Microwave Time on Medium (275 Watts) Room Temperature	Frozen
Bagels (4" diameter)	1	2	35 to 40 sec [60 to 70 sec]	1 to 1¼ min [1¾ to 2 min]
Biscuits (2" diameter)	1	2	15 to 20 sec [20 to 25 sec]	40 to 45 sec [1¼ to 1½ min]
Bread slices (from 1-lb loaf)	2 (stacked)	4 (2 stacks)	———	30 to 35 sec [55 to 60 sec]
Buns, hamburger	1	2	20 to 25 sec [50 to 55 sec]	40 to 45 sec [1 to 1¼ min]
Coffee cake (2½" wedge)	1	2	30 to 35 sec [50 to 55 sec]	45 to 55 sec [1¼ to 1½ min]
Croissants	1	2	20 to 25 sec [35 to 50 sec]	45 to 55 sec [1¼ to 1½ min]
Muffins (2½" diameter in paper baking cups)	1	2	15 to 20 sec [25 to 30 sec]	40 to 45 sec [1 to 1¼ min]
Pita bread (6" diameter)	1	2 (stacked)	25 to 30 sec [50 to 60 sec]	50 to 60 sec [1½ to 1¾ min]
Rolls, dinner	1	2	15 to 20 sec [25 to 30 sec]	30 to 35 sec [50 to 60 sec]
Tortillas, corn or flour	2 (stacked)	4 (2 stacks)	15 to 20 sec [25 to 30 sec]	———

Snacks & Sweets

Rumaki

1 Serving	[2 Servings]
3 chicken livers (2 oz)	6 chicken livers (4 oz)
3 water chestnuts	6 water chestnuts
1 tbsp soy sauce	2 tbsp soy sauce
1½ tsp packed brown sugar	1 tbsp packed brown sugar
Dash of ground ginger	⅛ tsp ground ginger
½ small clove garlic, crushed	1 small clove garlic, crushed
3 slices bacon, cut into halves	6 slices bacon, cut into halves

Cut chicken livers into halves; cut water chestnuts crosswise into halves. Mix remaining ingredients except bacon in 10-oz casserole [**22-oz casserole**]. Stir in liver and water chestnuts, coating all sides. Cover and refrigerate at least 2 hours; drain.

Wrap piece of liver and piece of water chestnut in each bacon piece. Secure with wooden pick. Arrange on rack in 11 × 7 × 1½" dish. Cover with waxed paper and microwave on high (550 watts) 3 min [**4 min**]; turn rumaki over. Cover with waxed paper and microwave until bacon is crisp, 3 to 6 min longer [**6 to 10 min longer**]. Serve with sweet and sour sauce if desired.

Wine-marinated Shrimp

1 Serving	[2 Servings]
¼ cup dry white wine	½ cup dry white wine
1 tbsp lemon juice	2 tbsp lemon juice
⅛ tsp salt	¼ tsp salt
Dash of ground ginger	⅛ tsp ground ginger
½ small clove garlic, finely chopped	1 small clove garlic, finely chopped
4 oz deveined and peeled large shrimp	8 oz deveined and peeled large shrimp

Mix all ingredients except shrimp in 22-oz casserole [**1-qt casserole**]. Cover tightly and microwave on high (550 watts) until boiling, 1½ to 2 min [**2½ to 3 min**]. Add shrimp, coating all sides. Cover tightly and microwave until shrimp is done, 45 sec to 1¼ min [**45 sec to 1¼ min**]. Cover and refrigerate in marinade 3 hours. Drain; serve with seafood cocktail sauce and wooden picks if desired.

Clockwise from top: Assorted Relishes, Rumaki, Wine-marinated Shrimp

Garlic-Swiss Mushrooms

1 Serving	[2 Servings]
2 large mushrooms	4 large mushrooms
½ tsp margarine or butter	1 tsp margarine or butter
2 tbsp soft bread crumbs	¼ cup soft bread crumbs
1 tbsp shredded Swiss cheese	2 tbsp shredded Swiss cheese
¼ tsp lemon juice	½ tsp lemon juice
⅛ tsp snipped parsley	¼ tsp snipped parsley
Dash of garlic power	⅛ tsp garlic power
Dash of salt	Dash of salt
Dash of pepper	Dash of pepper
Paprika	Paprika

Cut stems from mushrooms; finely chop stems. Place stems and margarine in 1-cup measure [2-cup measure]. Microwave uncovered on high (550 watts) until tender, 30 to 45 sec [45 to 60 sec]. Stir in remaining ingredients except paprika.

Fill mushroom caps with stuffing; arrange in circle on small plate. Microwave uncovered on high (550 watts) until hot, 45 to 60 sec [2 to 2½ min]. Sprinkle with paprika.

Green Onion Crackers

1 Serving	[2 Servings]
1½ tsp mayonnaise or salad dressing	1 tbsp mayonnaise or salad dressing
Dash of garlic powder	⅛ tsp garlic powder
Dash of white pepper	⅛ tsp white pepper
1 tbsp shredded mozzarella cheese	2 tbsp shredded mozzarella cheese
1 green onion (with top), thinly sliced	2 green onions (with tops), thinly sliced
5 round buttery crackers	10 round buttery crackers

Mix mayonnaise, garlic powder and pepper. Stir in cheese and onions[s]. Mound about 1 tsp onion mixture on each cracker. Arrange crackers in circle on plate. Microwave uncovered on high (550 watts) until cheese is melted, about 30 sec [about 45 sec].

Garlic-Swiss Mushrooms

Tiny Barbecued Ribs

1 Serving	[2 Servings]
½ lb spareribs, cut across bones into halves	1 lb spareribs, cut across bones into halves
1 tbsp soy sauce	2 tbsp soy sauce
1 tbsp chili sauce	2 tbsp chili sauce
1½ tsp packed brown sugar	1 tbsp packed brown sugar
1½ tsp dry white wine	1 tbsp dry white wine
½ small clove garlic, finely chopped	1 small clove garlic, finely chopped

Cut spareribs between each rib into individual pieces. Place ribs, meaty sides up, in 11 × 7 × 1½" dish. Mix remaining ingredients; spoon over ribs. Cover and refrigerate at least 2 hours.

Cover ribs with waxed paper and microwave on high (550 watts) 3 min [**4 min**]; rotate dish ½ turn. Microwave until ribs are done, 2 to 4 min longer [**5 to 9 min longer**].

Bacon Bites with Barbecue Dip

1 Serving	[2 Servings]
2 tbsp catsup	¼ cup catsup
1 tsp packed brown sugar	2 tsp packed brown sugar
1 tsp finely chopped onion	2 tsp finely chopped onion
Dash of garlic powder	⅛ tsp garlic powder
Dash of dry mustard	⅛ tsp dry mustard
Dash of Worcestershire sauce	⅛ tsp Worcestershire sauce
One ¾"-thick slice Canadian-style bacon (2 oz)	Two ¾"-thick slices Canadian-style bacon (2 oz each)

Mix all ingredients except Canadian-style bacon in ½-cup serving dish. Cover loosely and microwave on high (550 watts) until hot, 20 to 30 sec [**30 to 45 sec**]; stir.

Cut bacon into ¾" pieces. Skewer each on wooden pick and arrange in 12-oz casserole [**22-oz casserole**]. Cover loosely and microwave on medium-high (385 watts) until hot, 45 sec to 1¼ min [**2½ to 3 min**]. Serve with dip.

111

Mexican-style Dip

1 Serving	[2 Servings]
1 tsp margarine or butter	2 tsp margarine or butter
1/4 small clove garlic, finely chopped	1/2 small clove garlic, finely chopped
1/4 cup shredded sharp process American cheese	1/2 cup shredded sharp process American cheese
2 tbsp medium salsa	1/4 cup medium salsa
Dash of chili powder	1/8 tsp chili powder
Corn chips or green pepper, zucchini and celery sticks	Corn chips or green pepper, zucchini and celery sticks

Place margarine and garlic in 6-oz custard cup **[10-oz custard cup]**. Microwave uncovered on high (550 watts) until garlic is soft, 30 to 45 sec **[1 to 1¼ min]**. Stir in cheese, salsa and chili powder. Microwave uncovered on medium (275 watts) until cheese is melted, 1 to 1¼ min **[1¾ to 2¼ min]**; stir. Serve with corn chips or vegetable sticks.

Hot Horseradish Dip

1 Serving	[2 Servings]
1/2 pkg (3-oz size) cream cheese	1 pkg (3 oz) cream cheese
1 tsp prepared horseradish	2 tsp prepared horseradish
3 drops red pepper sauce	6 drops red pepper sauce
Dash of salt	Dash of salt
Snipped chives	Snipped chives
Uncooked vegetables	Uncooked vegetables

Place cream cheese in 6-oz custard cup **[10-oz custard cup]**. Microwave uncovered on medium (275 watts) until softened, 20 to 30 sec **[40 to 50 sec]**. Stir in horseradish, pepper sauce and salt. Microwave uncovered on high (550 watts) until hot, 20 to 30 sec **[40 to 50 sec]**; stir. Sprinkle with chives. Serve with vegetables.

Cheesy Sausage Chips

1 Serving	[2 Servings]
8 tortilla chips	16 tortilla chips
2 tbsp finely chopped pepperoni	1/4 cup finely chopped pepperoni
3 tbsp shredded hot pepper cheese or mozzarella cheese	1/3 cup shredded hot pepper cheese or mozzarella cheese

Place tortilla chips in single layer on 6" plate **[8" plate]**. Sprinkle chopped pepperoni and shredded cheese evenly over chips. Microwave uncovered on medium (275 watts) until cheese is melted, 30 to 45 sec **[1 to 1½ min]**.

CRISP VEGETABLES TO SERVE WITH DIPS

Asparagus spears
Broccoli flowerets
Carrot sticks
Cauliflowerets
Celery sticks
Cherry tomatoes
Cucumber spears
Daikon circles
Kohlrabi spears
Small mushrooms
Green onions
Sugar peas
Green and red pepper slices
Red and white radishes
Zucchini circles

Mexican-style Dip, Hot Horseradish Dip

Caramel-Granola Candies

1 Serving	[2 Servings]
Prepare Caramel-Granola Candies for 2 servings. Cover and refrigerate remaining candies.	**6 vanilla caramel candies**
	³⁄₄ tsp water
	¹⁄₂ cup granola
	2 tbsp semisweet chocolate chips
	Chopped pecans, if desired

Place caramels and water in 1-cup measure. Microwave uncovered on high (550 watts) 30 sec; stir. Microwave uncovered until melted, 10 to 20 sec longer. Stir until smooth; mix in granola. Drop by teaspoonfuls onto waxed paper. Refrigerate until firm, about 30 min.

Place chocolate chips in 6-oz custard cup. Microwave uncovered on medium (275 watts) until softened, 2¹⁄₂ to 3 min; stir until smooth. Spread over each caramel; sprinkle with chopped pecans. Refrigerate until chocolate is firm, about 15 min.

Chocolate-Pecan Clusters

1 Serving	[2 Servings]
Prepare Chocolate-Pecan Clusters for 2 Servings. Store remaining clusters in airtight container.	**¹⁄₂ cup miniature marshmallows**
	¹⁄₄ cup semisweet chocolate chips
	1 tbsp margarine or butter
	¹⁄₈ tsp vanilla
	¹⁄₃ cup small whole pecans

Place marshmallows, chocolate chips and margarine in 1-qt casserole. Cover tightly and microwave on high (550 watts) 30 sec; stir. Cover and microwave until mixture can be stirred smooth, 30 to 45 sec longer. Stir in vanilla and pecans. Drop by teaspoonfuls onto waxed paper. Refrigerate until firm, about 30 min.

Caramel-Granola Candies

Peanut-Popcorn Balls

1 Serving	**[2 Servings]**
Prepare Peanut-Popcorn Balls for 2 servings. Store remaining ball in plastic wrap.	**2 tbsp packed brown sugar**
	2 tbsp corn syrup
	1 tbsp creamy peanut butter
	Dash of salt
	2 cups popped popcorn
	¼ cup salted peanuts

Mix brown sugar, corn syrup, peanut butter and salt in 1-qt casserole. Microwave uncovered on high (550 watts) until mixture begins to bubble, 30 to 45 sec; stir. Stir in popcorn and peanuts until well coated. Cool 5 min. Shape mixture firmly into two 3" balls with hands dipped in cold water. Place on waxed paper; cool completely. Wrap each popcorn ball in plastic wrap.

Caramel-Cinnamon Apples

1 Serving	**[2 Servings]**
Prepare Caramel-Cinnamon Apples. Store remaining apple in waxed paper.	**2 medium apples**
	2 wooden skewers or ice-cream sticks
	12 vanilla caramel candies
	1½ tsp water
	¼ tsp ground cinnamon
	1 tbsp finely chopped pecans

Remove stems and blossom ends of apples (make sure apples are completely dry). Insert wooden skewer in stem end of each apple.

Place caramels, water and cinnamon in 2-cup measure. Microwave uncovered on high (550 watts), stirring every 30 sec, until melted, 1 to 1¼ min. Stir until smooth. Dip each apple into caramel mixture, turning apple and tilting measure, if necessary, to coat completely. Press bottoms of apples in pecans. Place on waxed paper. Refrigerate until coating is firm, about 20 min.

115

Spicy Nuts

1 Serving	[2 Servings]
1/4 cup pecan or walnut halves	1/2 cup pecan or walnut halves
1/8 tsp salt	1/4 tsp salt
1/8 tsp ground ginger	1/4 tsp ground ginger
Dash of ground nutmeg	1/8 tsp ground nutmeg
1 tsp margarine or butter	2 tsp margarine or butter

Place pecans in 10-oz casserole [22-oz casserole]. Sprinkle with salt, ginger and nutmeg; dot with margarine. Microwave uncovered on high (550 watts) until pecans are hot, 45 sec to 1¼ min [1¼ to 2 min]; stir. Serve warm.

Spiced Tea

1 Serving	[2 Servings]
3/4 cup hot water	1½ cups hot water
1½ tsp sugar	1 tbsp sugar
1 tsp instant tea	2 tsp instant tea
Dash of ground allspice	1/8 tsp ground allspice
Dash of ground cloves	Dash of ground cloves

Mix all ingredients in 2-cup measure [4-cup measure]. Microwave uncovered on high (550 watts) until hot, 1¼ to 2 min [2½ to 4 min]. Garnish with quarter of orange slice that has whole clove inserted in edge if desired.

Hot Chocolate

1 Serving	[2 Servings]
1/4 cup hot water	1/2 cup hot water
1 tbsp sugar	2 tbsp sugar
Dash of salt	Dash of salt
1/2 square (1/2 oz) unsweetened chocolate	1 square (1 oz) unsweetened chocolate
3/4 cup milk	1½ cups milk

Mix water, sugar and salt in 2-cup measure [4-cup measure]; add chocolate. Cover tightly and microwave on high (550 watts) until chocolate can be stirred smooth, 45 to 60 sec [1¼ to 2 min]. Stir in milk. Microwave uncovered until hot (do not boil), 1¾ to 2½ min [3½ to 5 min]. Beat with wire whisk until foamy. Garnish with whipped cream and fresh grated nutmeg if desired.

Mulled Wine

1 Serving	[2 Servings]
1/2 cup dry red wine	1 cup dry red wine
1/4 cup hot water	1/2 cup hot water
1 tbsp packed brown sugar	2 tbsp packed brown sugar
1/4 tsp grated orange peel	1/2 tsp grated orange peel
1/8 tsp ground cinnamon	1/4 tsp ground cinnamon
1/8 tsp ground cloves	1/4 tsp ground cloves

Mix all ingredients in 2-cup measure [4-cup measure]. Cover tightly and microwave on high (550 watts) until boiling, 1½ to 2½ min [2 to 3 min]. Strain; serve with cinnamon stick[s] if desired.

Apple Crisp

1 Serving	[2 Servings]
¾ cup sliced tart apples	1½ cups sliced tart apples
1 tbsp all-purpose flour	2 tbsp all-purpose flour
1 tbsp quick-cooking oats	2 tbsp quick-cooking oats
1 tbsp packed brown sugar	2 tbsp packed brown sugar
1 tbsp margarine or butter, softened	2 tbsp margarine or butter, softened
Dash of ground cinnamon	⅛ tsp ground cinnamon
Dash of ground nutmeg	⅛ tsp ground nutmeg

Spread apples in 12-oz casserole [**24-oz casserole**]. Mix remaining ingredients until crumbly; sprinkle over apples. Microwave uncovered on high (550 watts) until apples are tender, 3 to 3½ min [**5 to 6 min**]. Serve warm with cinnamon or vanilla ice cream, if desired.

Honey-Spice Apple

1 Serving	[2 Servings]
1 medium baking apple	2 medium baking apples
1 tbsp raisins	2 tbsp raisins
1 tbsp honey	2 tbsp honey
⅛ tsp ground cinnamon	¼ tsp ground cinnamon
1 tsp margarine or butter	2 tsp margarine or butter

Core apple[**s**] and pare 1" strip of skin from around middle[**s**] to prevent splitting. Place apple[**s**] in 10-oz custard cup [**two 10-oz custard cups**]. Pack raisins into apple[**s**]. Mix honey and cinnamon; pour into apple[**s**]. Top with margarine. Cover tightly and microwave on high (550 watts) until skin is tender when pierced with fork, 2 to 2½ min [**3 to 4 min**]. Serve warm with cream if desired.

Apple Crisp

Blueberry Cobbler

1 Serving	[2 Servings]
1 tbsp sugar	2 tbsp sugar
1/2 tsp cornstarch	1 tsp cornstarch
2/3 cup fresh or frozen (thawed) blueberries	1 1/3 cups fresh or frozen(thawed) blueberries
1 tsp lemon juice	2 tsp lemon juice
1/4 cup buttermilk baking mix	1/2 cup buttermilk baking mix
1 tsp sugar	2 tsp sugar
1 tbsp milk	2 tbsp milk
1 tbsp dairy sour cream	2 tbsp dairy sour cream
1/2 tsp sugar	1 tsp sugar
Dash of ground cinnamon	1/8 tsp ground cinnamon

Mix 1 tbsp [2 tbsp] sugar and the cornstarch in 16-oz casserole [1-qt casserole]. Stir in blueberries and lemon juice. Microwave uncovered on medium-high (385 watts) until boiling, 2 to 3 1/2 min [3 1/2 to 6 1/2 min]; stir.

Mix baking mix, 1 tsp [2 tsp] sugar, the milk and sour cream until soft dough forms. Drop dough by 3 [6] spoonfuls onto hot blueberry mixture. Mix 1/2 tsp [1 tsp] sugar and the cinnamon; sprinkle over dough. Microwave uncovered until top of dough is almost dry, 1 1/2 to 3 min [2 1/2 to 4 1/2 min]. Let stand uncovered 5 min before serving.

Flaming Pecan Bananas

1 Serving	[2 Servings]
1 1/2 tsp margarine or butter	1 tbsp margarine or butter
1 1/2 tsp honey	1 tbsp honey
Dash of ground nutmeg	1/8 tsp ground nutmeg
1/2 firm banana, cut lengthwise into halves	1 firm banana, cut lengthwise into halves
1 1/2 tsp chopped pecans	1 tbsp chopped pecans
1 1/2 tsp dark rum	1 tbsp dark rum

Place margarine in 12-oz casserole. Microwave uncovered on high (550 watts) until melted, 10 to 20 sec [25 to 30 sec]. Stir in honey and nutmeg. Place

banana in honey mixture; roll to coat. Sprinkle with pecans. Microwave uncovered until hot, 30 to 60 sec [1 to 2 min].

Place rum in 1-cup measure. Microwave uncovered on high (550 watts) until warm, about 10 sec [about 15 sec]. Pour rum into metal serving spoon; ignite in spoon and pour over bananas.

Pear with Raspberry Sauce

1 Serving	[2 Servings]
1 firm large pear	2 firm large pears
1 tsp honey	2 tsp honey
1 tsp lemon juice	2 tsp lemon juice
1 tbsp raspberry preserves	2 tbsp raspberry preserves
1/4 cup frozen raspberries, thawed (reserve 1 tbsp syrup)	1/2 cup frozen raspberries, thawed (reserve 2 tbsp syrup)
1 tbsp brandy	2 tbsp brandy

Core pear[s] and pare skin from upper half to prevent splitting. Place pear[s] in 10-oz custard cup [two 10-oz custard cups]. Mix honey and lemon juice; pour over pear[s]. Cover tightly and microwave on high (550 watts) until almost tender when skin is pierced with fork, 3 to 4 min [5 to 6 min]. Remove from juices and place in serving dish[es].

Mix preserves and reserved raspberry syrup in 1-cup measure. Microwave uncovered on medium (275 watts) until warm, 20 to 30 sec [45 to 60 sec]; cool to room temperature. Stir in raspberries and brandy. Pour over warm pear[s].

Blueberry Cobbler

Chocolate-frosted Fruit and Nuts

1 Serving	[2 Servings]
2 tbsp semisweet chocolate chips	¼ cup semisweet chocolate chips
2 large strawberries (with caps)	4 large strawberries (with caps)
2 large dried apricots	4 large dried apricots
2 Brazil nuts	4 Brazil nuts

Place chocolate chips in 6-oz custard cup. Microwave uncovered on medium (275 watts) until softened, 2 to 2½ min [3 to 3½ min]; stir until smooth. Cover each strawberry, apricot and nut ⅔ of the way with melted chocolate; place on waxed paper. Refrigerate uncovered until chocolate is firm, no longer than 1 hr.

Dried Fruit Compote

1 Serving	[2 Servings]
8 dried apricots, cut into fourths	16 dried apricots, cut into fourths
4 dried figs, cut into fourths	8 dried figs, cut into fourths
1 tbsp raisins	2 tbsp raisins
¼ cup applesauce	½ cup applesauce
¼ cup water	½ cup water
1 tsp lemon juice	2 tsp lemon juice
Dash of ground ginger	⅛ tsp ground ginger

Mix all ingredients in 12-oz casserole [22-oz casserole]. Cover tightly and microwave on high (550 watts) 1 min [2 min]; stir. Cover tightly and microwave until fruit is tender when pierced with fork, 30 to 60 sec longer [1 to 2 min longer]. Cover and let stand 15 min [30 min]. Serve with whipped cream and freshly grated nutmeg if desired.

Strawberry-topped Cheesecakes

1 Serving	[2 Servings]
Prepare Strawberry-topped Cheesecakes for 2 Servings. Cover and refrigerate remaining cheesecake for another meal.	**1 tbsp margarine or butter**
	¼ cup graham cracker crumbs
	2 tsp sugar
	1 pkg (3 oz) cream cheese, softened
	¼ cup sugar
	¼ tsp vanilla
	1 egg
	1 tbsp strawberry preserves
	1 tbsp dairy sour cream
	3 drops red food color
	2 strawberries

Place margarine in small bowl. Microwave uncovered on high (550 watts) until melted, 25 to 30 sec. Stir in crumbs and 2 tsp sugar with fork. Divide evenly between two 6-oz custard cups. Press mixture firmly and evenly on bottoms and sides of cups. Microwave uncovered on high (550 watts) until set, 45 to 60 sec.

Place cream cheese, ¼ cup sugar, the vanilla and egg in small bowl. Beat on high speed until smooth, about 1½ min. Divide mixture evenly between crusts. Microwave uncovered on medium (275 watts) until centers are almost set, 2½ to 3½ min. (Tops will not look completely done.)

Mix preserves, sour cream and food color; spread carefully over fillings. Cover and refrigerate until chilled, at least 1 hr. Just before serving, cut strawberries 3 to 4 times from points to stem ends; fan slices. Garnish cheesecakes with strawberry fans.

Strawberry-topped Cheesecakes

Mocha Mousse

1 Serving	**[2 Servings]**
Prepare Mocha Mousse for 2 Servings. Cover and refrigerate remaining mousse for another meal.	**1 tbsp sugar**
	1 tsp cornstarch
	½ cup chilled whipping cream
	2 tbsp semisweet chocolate chips
	1 tbsp coffee liqueur

Mix sugar and cornstarch in 2-cup measure; gradually mix ¼ cup of the cream. Stir in chocolate chips. Microwave uncovered on medium (275 watts), stirring every 30 sec, until chocolate is softened, 1 to 1½ min. Stir in liqueur. Refrigerate until chilled, about 30 min.

Beat remaining cream in chilled bowl until soft peaks form; fold chilled chocolate mixture into whipped cream. Pour into 2 small soufflé dishes. Cover and refrigerate at least 1½ hours before serving. Garnish with chocolate curls if desired.

Strawberry Shortcake

1 Serving	**[2 Servings]**
2 tsp packed brown sugar	**1 tbsp plus 1 tsp packed brown sugar**
1 tsp cornstarch	**2 tsp cornstarch**
3 tbsp water	**¼ cup plus 2 tbsp water**
1 tbsp orange liqueur	**2 tbsp orange liqueur**
1 drop red food color	**2 drops red food color**
1 shortcake	**2 shortcakes**
1 cup strawberries, cut into halves	**2 cups strawberries, cut into halves**
2 tbsp whipped cream	**¼ cup whipped cream**

Mix brown sugar and cornstarch in 1-cup measure **[2-cup measure]**. Stir in water, liqueur and food color. Microwave uncovered on high (550 watts) until boiling, 30 to 45 sec **[1 to 1¼ min]**. Cover and refrigerate until cool, about 20 min **[about 40 min]**.

Stir strawberries into sauce. Fill shortcake**[s]** with strawberry mixture. Top with whipped cream.

Mocha Mousse

Hot Fudge Sundae Cake

1 Serving	[2 Servings]
Prepare Hot Fudge Sundae Cake for 2 Servings. Cover and refrigerate half of the cake for another meal.	*¼ cup all-purpose flour* *3 tbsp granulated sugar* *2 tsp cocoa* *½ tsp baking powder* *Dash of salt* *2 tbsp milk* *2 tsp vegetable oil* *¼ tsp vanilla* *2 tbsp chopped nuts* *¼ cup packed brown sugar* *1 tbsp cocoa* *½ cup hot water* *Ice cream*

Mix flour, granulated sugar, 2 tsp cocoa, the baking powder and salt in 24-oz casserole. Stir in milk, oil and vanilla until smooth. Stir in nuts; sprinkle with brown sugar and 1 tbsp cocoa.

Place water in 1-cup measure. Microwave uncovered on high (550 watts) until boiling, 1 to 1½ min. Pour over batter. Microwave uncovered on high (550 watts) 1 min; rotate casserole ¼ turn. Microwave uncovered until cake is set but still glossy, 1½ to 2 min longer. Serve warm topped with scoops of ice cream. Garnish with sliced bananas, toasted nuts and maraschino cherries if desired.

Deep-Dish Chocolate Chip Brownies

1 Serving	[2 Servings]
Prepare Deep-Dish Chocolate Chip Brownies for 2 Servings. Store half of the brownies in airtight container for another meal.	*¼ cup margarine or butter* *½ cup sugar* *½ cup all-purpose flour* *2 tbsp cocoa* *½ tsp baking powder* *½ tsp mint flavoring or vanilla* *⅛ tsp salt* *1 egg* *¼ cup semisweet chocolate chips*

Place margarine in 6¼ × 5¼ × 1½" dish. Microwave uncovered on medium-high (385 watts) until melted, 1 to 1½ min. Mix in sugar, flour, cocoa, baking powder, mint flavoring, salt and egg. Stir in chocolate chips. Spread batter evenly in dish. Place dish on inverted plate in microwave oven. Microwave uncovered on medium (275 watts) 2 min; rotate dish ¼ turn. Microwave uncovered, rotating dish ¼ turn every 2 min, until wooden pick inserted about 1" from center comes out clean, 2 to 6 min longer.

Let stand on flat, heatproof surface until completely cool (do not use wire rack). Cut into bars, about 1½ × 1¼".

Apricot Brandy Sauce, Chocolate-Peppermint Topping

Apricot Brandy Sauce

1 Serving	[2 Servings]
Prepare Apricot Brandy Sauce for 2 Servings. Store remaining sauce in refrigerator. Reheat sauce on medium (275 watts) until warm.	1/4 **cup apricot preserves** 1 **tbsp corn syrup** 1 **tsp lemon juice** 1 **tbsp apricot-flavored brandy**

Mix jam, corn syrup, and lemon juice in 1-cup measure. Microwave uncovered on high (550 watts) until jam is melted, 30 to 40 sec. Stir in brandy. Serve warm over pound cake or ice cream.

Chocolate-Peppermint Topping

1 Serving	[2 Servings]
Prepare Chocolate-Peppermint Topping for 2 Servings. Cover and refrigerate half of the sauce. To reheat, microwave uncovered on medium (275 watts) until warm.	2 **tbsp sugar** 3 **tbsp whipping cream** 1/3 **cup semisweet chocolate chips** 1/4 **tsp peppermint extract**

Mix sugar and cream in 1-cup measure. Stir in chocolate chips. Microwave uncovered on medium (275 watts) until chocolate is softened, 1½ to 2 min. Stir in peppermint extract until smooth. Serve warm over ice cream or other desserts.

Lemon Dessert Sauce, Butterscotch-Ginger Sauce

Lemon Dessert Sauce

1 Serving	[2 Servings]
Prepare Lemon Dessert Sauce for 2 Servings. Store remaining sauce in refrigerator. Reheat sauce on medium (275 watts) until warm.	**2 tbsp sugar** **1 tsp cornstarch** **¼ cup water** **1 tbsp lemon juice** **½ tsp grated lemon peel** **Dash of salt** **1½ tsp margarine or butter**

Mix sugar and cornstarch in 1-cup measure; stir in water, lemon juice, lemon peel and salt. Microwave uncovered on high (550 watts) stirring every 30 sec, until thickened and boiling, 1 to 1½ min. Stir in margarine until smooth. Serve warm over gingerbread, steamed pudding or cake.

Butterscotch-Ginger Sauce

1 Serving	[2 Servings]
Prepare Butterscotch-Ginger Sauce for 2 Servings. Cover and refrigerate half of the sauce. To reheat, microwave uncovered on medium (275 watts) until warm.	**⅓ cup packed brown sugar** **2 tsp cornstarch** **¼ tsp ground ginger** **3 tbsp honey** **¼ cup half-and-half** **1 tbsp margarine or butter** **2 tbsp finely chopped crystallized ginger**

Mix brown sugar, cornstarch and ground ginger in 2-cup measure. Mix in honey. Stir in half-and-half and margarine. Microwave uncovered on high (550 watts), stirring every min, until thickened, 2 to 2½ min. Stir in crystallized ginger. Serve warm over ice cream.

Index

126